CHAMPIONS

OF

COLLABORATIVE

DIVORCE

CHANGING THE WAY
THE WORLD GETS DIVORCED

VOLUME I - TAMPA BAY

AN ANTHOLOGY
EDITED BY JORYN JENKINS

CHAMPIONS OF COLLABORATIVE DIVORCE, CHANGING THE WAY THE WORLD GETS DIVORCED (VOLUME I - TAMPA BAY)

Published by Open Palm Press
Copyright © 2017 by Joryn Jenkins
Cover art by 4EDGE, LLC

First Printing: April 2017
Printed in the United States of America

First Edition: April 2017

TABLE OF CONTENTS

INTRODUCTION

The collaborative approach is revolutionizing the way in which people get divorced. Tired of watching already fragile families being utterly destroyed in traditional courtroom divorces, collaborative pioneer Stuart Webb founded collaborative divorce, a family-centric process intended to resolve domestic disputes in a kinder, gentler fashion.

Simply speaking, couples who seek a collaborative resolution to their divorces retain a team of professionals who work together with them to find a resolution that considers the entire family's best interests. Each client is represented by his or her own attorney. The attorneys pledge to withdraw from representation if the clients are unable to reach an agreement. This disqualification provision gives the attorneys a vested interest in the collaborative approach because if they cannot help their clients reach an agreement, their engagement ends. They cannot represent the clients in litigation. It also eliminates the conflict of interest that attorneys and their clients have with one another as lawyers sometimes "stir the pot," either purposefully or unwittingly generating more fees for themselves.

The team also usually includes one or two communications specialists, mental health professionals of one kind or another who either run the meetings in the one-coach model or act as personal coaches to the clients in the two-coach model. These facilitators are invaluable members of the team, teaching clients how to better communicate, brainstorm, problem-solve, and co-parent, skills that they certainly do *not* learn when litigating. Facilitators not only coach the clients, but they also help the entire team work together and function at each member's highest level.

If a child specialist is not included on the team, facilitators also

1

work with parents to develop their parenting plans. They are better situated than the lawyers to do so as most are trained in the developmental stages of children, and they bill at lower hourly rates, saving the entire family money.

Collaborative teams may also include a neutral financial professional who helps the clients compile financial information about their assets, liabilities, and budgets, prepare financial affidavits and schedules, and formulate settlement options. These team members also tend to bill at lower hourly rates than the attorneys, and, like the facilitators, they are better equipped to perform these tasks than the lawyers are.

In all of their work, collaborative professionals guide clients through interest-based, rather than position-based negotiations. This style of negotiation opens up many more potential and reasonable outcomes for families because, rather than becoming stuck in fighting for a specific position, clients determine what their true interests are behind their positions. For example, a position would be, "I want to stay in the marital home," while an interest is, "I want to maintain as much stability for my children as possible, and not forcing them to move would help maintain that stability," or "I want a house in the neighborhood where all my kids' friends live." When arguing over the position of staying in the marital home, there is only one option that wins . . . staying in the marital home. But if the clients can negotiate the underlying goal or interest instead, there are numerous options, like moving to another home in the same school district or in the same neighborhood.

At the beginning of the process, clients are asked to identify their most important interests, and throughout the collaborative discussions, team members remind them of those goals and work together to help satisfy each client's most critical concerns.

The advantages of the collaborative process over conventional litigation are abundant. In a divorce in which minor children are involved, where the couple earns over $100,000 annually and assets and liabilities must be distributed, and in which support is in question, a collaborative divorce will cost a couple tens of thousands of dollars less than a litigated divorce.

In litigation, attorneys play expensive "discovery" games, making it difficult for either party to feel comfortable that all important information has been disclosed. Yet, in a collaborative divorce, clients pledge to be transparent, saving themselves money and giving themselves peace of mind that they have the appropriate information necessary to enter into important agreements.

While a litigated divorce case may take years to resolve and often spawns years of post-judgment conflict both in and out of court, collaborative teams work together to move matters along quickly, often resolving matters within six months.

In a litigated divorce, personal matters become part of the public court file. In collaboration, only "bare bones" agreements and financial affidavits are filed, thus keeping private matters private.

Rather than a judge who doesn't know the spouses or their children or who doesn't necessarily share their values deciding a family's fate, clients take a front seat in making the decisions that will forever change their lives. Instead of putting children in the middle of disputes, children are given a voice through child specialists. Parenting plans drafted by experts allow for their developmental stages as children mature into adults.

Collaborative teammates are often chosen by each other because they have worked well together in the past and they are comfortable with one another. They are what we call "trusted advisors." We "know, like, and trust each other" so that, when the client allows us to make the choice, we choose to work with each other.

Next Generation Divorce is a practice group of professionals, all of whom are dedicated to the collaborative approach to dissolution of marriage. The contributors to this book are all devoted members of this practice group in Tampa Bay, Florida. They are people I refer to as "Collaborative Champions," professionals who are in the forefront of pioneering this disruptive, yet constructive approach to a typically destructive life event.

Through this book, collaborative professionals can learn more about who each author is and what he or she stands for. I aim here, not just to introduce these collaborative champions to the public, but also to introduce these new voices in collaborative divorce to our world-wide community. Seasoned collaborative professionals should consider these authors when putting together collaborative teams in the future and couples seeking to divorce collaboratively should consider them when deciding whom to retain to serve on their collaborative divorce teams.

Joryn Jenkins
March 3, 2017, Tampa, Florida

There is magic in collaboration, magic that certainly is not found in litigation. Often times in a divorce, one side is more vulnerable than the other. It may be because a spouse has been victimized throughout the marriage, is less educated and/or knowledgeable than the other, is traveling more slowly through the stages of grief, suffers from poor physical health, has an addiction and/or mental disorder, or is experiencing difficulty for any number of other reasons. Whatever the cause, these couples are not on a level playing field during their divorce. Litigation only exacerbates the difference between them, making it difficult to actually reach a fair result and often leaving at least one spouse feeling utterly destroyed.

By contrast, a collaborative team envelops its clients with support and understanding that helps level the playing field and improves a family's chances of reaching an equitable resolution. Collaborative clients end their marriages with a new understanding of how to communicate, co-parent, and negotiate—skills that will help them going forward, not only with their exes but also in all of their present and future relationships. – Ed. Note

COLLABORATIVE OFFERS SO MUCH MORE THAN LITIGATION
BY FAITH Z. BROWN, ESQ.

Diane was a 58-year-old plain-looking woman with long brown hair and little makeup. When I met her for our initial consult, she wore a pair of old jeans with a flannel shirt. Her demeanor and appearance made it clear that she was not a person of means. She told me that she purchased her wardrobe at Goodwill.

An anxious woman with a seventh-grade education, she took several depression and anxiety medications, including Wellbutrin and Xanax. Both her psychiatrist and counselor recommended she seek a divorce. According to Diane, Jeff was a controlling narcissist.

Shaking, with her hands clasped together, she pleaded with me in a soft Southern lilt. "Please, you've got to help me. I can't do it anymore. I can't go on living with him, but he says I'm not entitled to anything."

She kept repeating, "I'm not smart. I only went to school through the seventh grade. That's when I got pregnant, and my mother told me to marry the guy."

After glancing at the notes my legal assistant had compiled during her initial phone call with Diane and verifying that she had no children with the man to whom she was currently married, I asked, "What happened to that husband?"

Shamefaced, she said, "We were just so young. Our relationship was doomed from the start, and we got divorced. But that left me a single mother with no high school diploma and no training. I was only 17."

"How long after that did you meet your current husband?"

"Many years later, after my daughter was already grown." She paused before she continued. "I know what it's like to be broke and desperate, and that's what scares me so much about this divorce. But I just can't stay in this marriage any longer. I don't have a job, and I don't know if I can live on my own, but I've got to get away from him."

"Why do you feel that way?"

"He's an alcoholic, and he's really mean to me. And it's only getting worse."

"Did something happen that made you realize you had to get a divorce now?"

She fought back tears. "He called the cops on me and claimed that I was getting violent towards him. He was drunk. When the sheriff arrived and Jeff didn't like how they were handling things, he called 911 and asked them to send new police officers who knew what they were doing because, obviously, the ones who were there didn't have a clue. One of the officers walked up to him while he was talking to the 911 dispatcher, overheard what he was saying, and arrested him for making a false report."

She paused to calm herself, although the tears had already started spilling. She took a breath. Her cheeks aflame, she quietly added, "And I bailed him out."

I handed her a tissue. "Can you get your hands on enough money to cover living expenses for a couple of months? He'll probably try to cut you off financially as soon as you file for divorce."

"I don't know. I've never dealt with the money, but I took some money out of the safe at the bank."

"How much did you take?"

"Two hundred thousand dollars. But I left over $400,000. The nice lady at the bank helped me open my own bank account with it."

As it turned out, Diane's husband, Jeff, was a 70-year-old retired nuclear engineer who had sold his business a year earlier for several million dollars and had started a new business that stood to make millions of dollars in the next couple of years.

"Tell me about your marriage."

"We've been married for 18 years, but together for over 25. We were happy for a long time. I was a traditional housewife, cooking, cleaning, and taking care of him. Meanwhile, he handled the money. He paid all the bills and gave me a $200 monthly allowance to buy groceries and any other items I wanted."

They lived in a million-dollar home on the golf course of a prestigious country club. They had a pool and a dog. Both had grown children from prior marriages.

"Tell me about your relationship with your daughter."

"I've always had a wonderful relationship with my daughter Ashley and granddaughter Denise. They live in New York City. But Jeff is estranged from all of his children except one, Blake."

"You say that you were happy for a while. What changed?"

"His social drinking became an everyday occurrence. I can't live like this any longer."

"What are your goals for your divorce and afterward?"

"I never want to have to worry about money again. I don't need to be rich, just comfortable. Jeff earned all this money, and I don't feel that it's right for me to get half. But I also contributed to the marriage, so I feel that I should be financially secure after our divorce. I know our marriage has taken a toll on me physically and emotionally, and I need it to be over. I don't want a long, drawn-out divorce. I just want what's fair."

If Diane's divorce had been a litigated case, her legal position with the court would have been that she was legally entitled to half, despite feeling that she was not morally entitled to it. Her mental health was deteriorating from the stress of living with Jeff and it was doubtful that she could handle the pressure of litigation. Testifying in court would also be difficult, if not impossible, for her.

With this in mind, we discussed her divorce options, including collaborative, and she took some time to consider the best way to proceed. Soon after our meeting, she retained my services.

I later learned that Jeff had started his business several years prior to meeting her and had had a net worth of approximately $10,000,000 at the time of their marriage. When they separated, he had increased that net worth to approximately $12,000,000.

During their marriage, Jeff had commingled and converted his premarital assets into their joint names. This, of course, boded well for my client. Additionally, he was unable to access documentation from the investment companies to show the value of his premarital assets at the time of marriage because the companies did not keep records for that length of time. The only documentation he had was a net worth form that he had filled out to apply for a loan almost 20 years prior.

If the case had gone to litigation, he would have had a difficult time showing that any portion of the monies was non-marital or that he deserved an unequal distribution of assets.

The solution for them, albeit for different reasons, was to approach their divorce negotiations collaboratively. I made that proposal to Jeff in a very respectful and carefully worded letter. I crafted it to ensure that he understood the decision was completely his and that he was in control and I also gave him enough information to realize that this approach would best suit him and his circumstances. He agreed and hired another collaborative attorney in my practice group (I had provided him with the website in my letter), Alma Foxworth. Alma and I agreed to include Dr. Donati as the facilitator and Justin Coleman as the financial planner on our collaborative services team.

Although the clients resided in the same home, Diane was extremely anxious about being in the room with Jeff when finances were being discussed. At the first meeting, she sat next to me and clenched my hand for support.

Jeff started off combatively. It seemed as though he assumed he was fighting all of us except Alma. Before we even addressed the divorce issues, he wanted to change the wording of the facilitator's and financial neutral's contracts. After much debate, he finally conceded and signed the retainer agreements.

Once the contracts and the collaborative participation agreement were signed, he began his bullying. "I don't know why we need to have so many meetings and waste so much time and money. I told Diane that I would buy her a house and she could keep the $200,000 that she took out of the safe."

Obviously, this was not a "fair" settlement, nor did it meet Diane's goal of never having to worry about money.

Jeff continued to look at her intently across the table and to reiterate, forcefully, "That's a lot of money, Diane. You can spend it on anything you want."

She was clearly intimidated and broke down. We had to take a break so she could calm herself and collect her thoughts. Dr. Donati and I stepped outside with her to get some fresh air.

"I don't know what to do. I just want this to be over. I just want this to be over," Diane repeated, over and over.

Dr. Donati told her to take some time to breathe. "You don't have to make any decisions today. You have a good attorney who is here to guide you. Let Justin collect all of the financial information before you make any decisions that are going to affect the rest of your life."

After about 15 minutes, Diane seemed to be back in control and we reconvened the meeting.

The remainder of our two-hour meeting centered on sharing the goals and interests that Diane and Jeff had already identified. We all agreed they should not discuss the divorce or terms of settlement outside of our meetings. It was clear he was in a position of power and could easily manipulate her.

Diane wanted to move out of the house immediately but was afraid she would not be able to locate a place suitable for her dog, whom she refused to leave behind. The dog was her number one priority. After much discussion, it was decided that she would locate a furnished house and rent for six months while we worked out the terms of a settlement. Justin would help set up a checking account and teach her how to pay her bills online each month.

Unfortunately, Diane was too upset to look for a rental home. Dr. Donati called her daily to assess her emotional state and determine if she needed anything. Almost daily, he had to calm Diane down in order to keep her from making a hasty decision to settle for almost nothing, just to "have it over."

Meanwhile, Jeff was working with Justin to determine all of their assets, list how they were acquired and titled, and assess their values.

At the second meeting, Jeff's attorney recommended and Jeff offered to immediately buy Diane a house as part of the settlement. With the assistance of a realtor friend, she located and fell in love with a home in Sarasota for $240,000. She immediately put in a cash offer and became obsessed with it.

Two days after she signed the contract on the house, Dr. Donati called me. Diane had told him that Jeff had demanded that she sign an agreement and assured her that he would take care of her.

What agreement? It seemed that Jeff had gone behind the team's back and written up an agreement that he then presented to Diane and insisted she sign. He told her that unless she signed it, he would not buy her the house. She was unemployed, so no lending institution would loan her the $40,000 she needed to complete the purchase on her own. She felt cornered.

I immediately called her. She told me Jeff had *assured* her that he would take care of her *if* she signed his agreement, which gave her virtually nothing. She reiterated that she was scared of him and just wanted it to be over, so she had signed his agreement.

With the assistance of Dr. Donati and Justin, we were able to convince Diane that it was not in her best interest to settle for Jeff's $500,000 offer.

After discussing the situation with all of the team professionals, Jeff's attorney contacted him and explained that the paper he had Diane sign was executed under duress and didn't meet the standard to qualify for a settlement agreement. Additionally, his attorney convinced him to finalize the purchase of the house so that Diane could move out of the marital residence.

Once Diane was out of the house, her stress and anxiety levels subsided, and we were able to start negotiating a deal that met everyone's goals.

CHAMPIONS OF COLLABORATIVE DIVORCE

As time progressed, Jeff put together a proposal with his attorney, which they submitted to me. After a quick review, my first reaction was to declare vehemently, "Absolutely not. Diane is entitled to a lot more."

But the collaborative process focuses on goals, not on positions, so I spoke with Justin, who reviewed the offer with me in depth. Jeff was offering Diane a little over $3,000,000 in settlement:

- $240,000 house
- $200,000 jewelry
- $1,500,000 in IRA
- $555,000 cash
- Range Rover
- '57 Chevy
- $10,000 for new furniture and appliances for Diane's new home
- A whole life policy with death benefit of $250,000 and current cash value of $122,000. Jeff would continue to pay the premiums.
- Lifetime permanent alimony that would survive Jeff's death in the amount of $4,700 per month. Upon Jeff's death, his estate would establish an annuity for Diane's benefit based on her life expectancy.
- Jeff would provide Diane with a policy that would cover home, health, or nursing home care in the event that Diane required such services in the future.

At first glance, it did not appear to be much, in light of their total net worth. After speaking with Justin and reviewing Diane's financial affidavit, however, it certainly met her goals. She would have no debt. When she splurged, she spent less than $1,500 per month on living expenses. She did not live, nor did she desire to live, an extravagant lifestyle.

Justin explained that, if she invested the cash conservatively, she could earn approximately $80,000 a year on the interest alone. She would go from being a woman with a $200 monthly allowance to a woman with $10,000 a month to spend, without touching her principal. Had this been a conventional courtroom divorce, the alimony would have ceased upon the death of the husband. The court would not have entertained the home health care policy. Nobody would have taught her how to invest her money or pay her bills. She would have been left with a large sum of money and probably would have ended up being taken advantage of financially.

We agreed to the offer.

Months later, I checked in on Diane to see how she was doing. Her mental health had improved dramatically since her divorce.

Happily, she said, "I no longer need to take Xanax regularly. Jeff and I have maintained a friendly relationship. He still calls me daily to tell me that he loves me and to wish me a good day. I call him for advice and for assistance with minor household repairs. He even dog sits for me on a regular basis!"

As this story illustrates, the collaborative process can offer so much more to a divorcing couple than litigation ever could, even when there are no minor children involved. I can only imagine how Diane's mental, physical, and financial states would have suffered if she and Jeff had litigated this divorce. Instead, these clients ended their marriage, meeting each of their most important goals and interests, and discovered that they were able to maintain a positive relationship with one another going forward because of it.

Faith Z. Brown is a trained family law collaborative attorney and VA-accredited attorney with over 11 years of extensive experience as a family law trial attorney. She is also effective at helping her clients negotiate agreements without the need to litigate before a judge.

Twice-divorced herself and the mother of three, Ms. Brown personally understands the difficulties and pitfalls of divorce. She has successfully navigated through the dissolution experience and maintains a positive relationship with her ex-husband, with whom she co-parents their two minor children.

Ms. Brown was the president of the Family Court Professional Collaborative in 2016 and chair of the 2015 and 2016 Family Court Professional Collaborative Conferences. She has been on their board of directors since 2014. She was the 2015 Vice President of the Collaborative Family Law Professionals of Sarasota/Manatee.

Ms. Brown was recognized by the Florida Bar Association and the State Supreme Court for her 2006 *pro bono* work in the area of family law. She has also been a member of the Keiser University Advisory Board since 2006.

Ms. Brown received her *Juris Doctor* from Loyola University New Orleans School of Law in 2003. She earned a bachelor's degree in English, Journalism, and Technical Writing from Southeastern Louisiana University. Prior to attending law school, Ms. Brown worked as a journalist in print, radio, and broadcast media.

You may reach Faith at FBrown@BrownAndBrown.Legal.

Collaborative practice is beneficial not only for its clients but also for the professionals who practice it. Trial attorneys, financial and other professionals who testify as experts at trial, and mental health professionals, who counsel those involved in marital and family distress, work in higher stress conditions than others do. Their stress is caused by the unpredictability of the judicial system, the heightened emotions of family law clients, the pressure sometimes to work in a way that may violate a professional's values and that may not appear to be in the best interest of the children, innocent bystanders, and the burdens placed on them by opposing counsels, judges, and employers. This stress can both lead to health issues and burnout, as well as affect the personal and family lives of the professionals themselves.

While collaboration does not completely alleviate the stress, working with a peaceful team of like-minded professionals provides a healthier, more enjoyable work environment. Because collaborative practice promotes equitable, holistic resolutions for the entire family, collaborative professionals feel better about the work they perform. Clients are happier and more supported, relieving the stress on the professionals who serve them. And when issues do arise, collaborative professionals can lean on one another and seek help from the professional on the team who specializes in whatever challenge is causing the issue, be it emotional, financial, or legal.

All of this means that collaborative professionals' work lives are typically far less stressful and more fulfilling than the lives of those who work with litigating clients. – Ed. Note

MEMOIR OF A COLLABORATIVE LAWYER: A PATH TO WELLNESS
BY GEORGE MELENDEZ, ESQ.

This is my journey, first as a soul, and, somewhat secondarily, as an attorney.

I vividly remember an almost transformative process unfolding as I entered and went through law school. After graduation, I felt lost, like a misplaced seed, fallen on a sidewalk. Rain would come, bits of soil would be tossed my way, but never the necessary nutrients to really thrive and grow.

I think many of us, lawyers especially, like to think we write our own destinies, that we are in control. But to be honest, even the most proactive of us have very little to do with determining where we eventually find ourselves.

Think about how each of our individual neurons came to be. Did we take our hands and place each connection within our brains? For example, words a grandparent said early in my childhood may have affected a choice I made later, that ultimately caused me to learn something, which was later reinforced and set into what is now considered the hardware of my brain. Tracking every encounter and experience is impossible. Instead, this memoir recollects some of those moments that have influenced my path to wellness and to becoming a better collaborative professional.

MY EDUCATION

As one privileged to attend Tampa's Jesuit High School, I give credit to the Jesuits with great pleasure. The Jesuits, more formally called *The Society of Jesus*, now usually referred to as *The Jesuits,* is a rather well-respected order of priests and brothers founded half a millennium ago by the soldier-turned-mystic Ignatius Loyola. It was through that education that I was taught and nurtured with the concept of "men and women for others."

I attended a liberal arts school, where I majored in studio fine art and minored in art history, choices unlikely to lead to a legal career.

Looking back, it is evident that each student eventually found his way through the program in a discipline that was influenced by his life experiences. It really didn't matter whether it was painting or sculpture or, in my case, ceramics. Our life experiences had real bearing on where we spent the majority of our time.

While in the art program, I vividly remember an intense period of discernment and introspective soul-searching when I called on

16

my inner self to surface. I was looking for the meaning of my own existence.

With my degree in hand, I sought my next direction by making art, teaching, and working various odd jobs. In addition, I began volunteering for the Guardian *Ad Litem* (GAL) Program.

The GAL Program uses professionals and volunteers to advocate for abused, abandoned, and neglected children. It is hard not to be motivated by the needs of these wonderful kids.

It is an honorable experience to advocate for children who have so little and who have endured so much. So, although I received a full scholarship from the University of Notre Dame Fine Arts Department, I turned it down and applied to law school. I wish I could wrap this up by saying that the rest is history, but it just ain't so. Although I found law school boring, there were some highlights. Eventually, I graduated and passed the bar.

This was the moment when the rubber met the road.

LITIGATION: THE SOLUTION TO NOWHERE

I found myself with bills and no experience or income, not unlike many new lawyers. (After we pass the bar, we are really only qualified to change light bulbs in a law office). Many new lawyers work for the State Attorney's Office, the Office of the Public Defender, or another governmental introductory job at which young lawyers learn how to litigate. In these jobs, they form habits and their legal personalities.

I eventually took a position with the Office of the Public Defender where, on my first day, my boss gave me a file to take to a certain room. That room happened to be the chambers of a judge who had just begun a restitution hearing against a defendant whom I was, apparently, to defend.

Clearly, I had been the subject of a prank, which, oh, by the way, happened to have bearing on the life of a real man. And I lost the hearing.

Work continued to humble and frustrate me. I was assigned a caseload of 300 clients for which I had ultimate authority with absolutely no instruction or guidance. I worked as a public defender in a circuit in which the Office of the State Attorney was not what most people would expect from the "Good Side." (We commonly referred to the State Attorney's Office as the "Dark Side.") My job was essentially to litigate against them.

During this period, I met many wonderful souls: people who had never had a chance in life, some who had things happen to them that excluded them from having any success, people whom the State of Florida considered garbage and who were systematically driven out of the county by either harassment or imprisonment.

After about a year, I was asked to move from Misdemeanors to Felonies (except those in which the State was seeking death). I quickly realized that I was not qualified for the job and questioned if anyone in the office was, except for a couple lead attorneys. How could anyone adequately represent hundreds of people?

We were supposed to give these indigent and unlucky souls hope. We tried, but we were outnumbered, and our office was the target of systematic bullying. It was disheartening, to say the least.

One of my clients spent four years in the county jail. The system, designed to move cases and either force or allow a plea deal or bring a case to trial for resolution by a judge or jury, failed. Four years in jail!

They forgot this man who had mental health conditions and whose crime was committed during a period of insanity when he did not appreciate the difference between right and wrong. I met him after he had spent over 1,400 days in the county jail. The jail staff knew he was there because they administered his daily medications, yet no one asked why he hadn't been seen by an attorney.

I was in litigation every day. At times, it was casual litigation in which we made plea bargains to settle matters in the middle of court. Other times, it was brutal, with heavy discovery culminating in hard-fought jury trials. The immense disparity of power was clear; the State had all the cards. Their entire prosecution was fully prepared by the time a public defender was appointed. The State had pretty much any resource at its fingertips, and they had the power to agree to a deal or to file more charges, whether new charges were justified or not.

The majority of the prosecutors followed the direction of one senior prosecutor in their office, and, as a result, prosecuted in a harsh, and at times, unprofessional manner. Other prosecutors, the minority, followed the direction of the other senior prosecutor and conducted themselves in a more professional manner with the goal to move the cases and to seek justice properly.

My experience as a public defender taught me that litigation almost always hurts. There was little opportunity to discuss the charges, the requests of the victims, or the defendant's possible rehabilitation. The State routinely refused to return calls, respond to correspondence, or discuss any case. It was all or nothing, and it wasn't nice.

To refuse a deal and to lose at trial ensured that your client was punished and frequently received the maximum sentence for taking the case to trial. The harsher sentence was not only intended to teach the defendant a lesson for challenging the State, but it was also meant to teach the public defender that he should not challenge the State or his clients would be punished. For those who were interested in their clients' wellbeing, this was a tough lesson.

Ultimately, the taxpayers paid because losing at trial meant more jail or prison time, for either of which they paid. The more the entire office was afraid to try cases, the more the State felt entitled to do whatever it wanted, including making up charges.

Assistant prosecutors were instructed that it wasn't their job to drop charges that were not legitimate or could not be proven. I remember taking a case to jury trial and winning . . . and later learning that my client had been harassed by the deputy on his way back to the holding cell after the jury found him not guilty.

My existence was consumed by stories of countless innocent souls who had only committed one crime, but who found themselves being falsely charged with three or four additional wrongdoings. I vividly remember meeting a man who had been tasered 17 times for no reason other than that the officer wanted to teach him a lesson.

One of my colleagues at the office decided to run for judge and had to put up with a negative campaign by an assistant prosecutor who posted hateful propaganda throughout the courthouse. After the prosecutor was chastised for his conduct, my friend was elected to the circuit court bench. By now I felt pressure in my chest and carotid arteries on the way to the office each morning. I knew that I needed to make a change.

That was my first three years as a practicing lawyer. I learned that the environment of pure litigation is detrimental to us all. Because there were few success stories, the outcomes bred distrust and animosity. Though this is a tale of my experience in criminal court, it reveals the type of litigation in which many lawyers receive their first training.

THE TRANSITION TO FAMILY LAW

When I decided to leave the public defender's office, I chose a job that was close to home. I was busy healing wounds, searching for options, and trying to breathe. My employer asked me to practice family law. I knew nothing about family law. I later learned that neither did my employer or anyone else at the office. Lawyers often hear the phrase "baptism by fire," which means learning by jumping in. Such was my introduction to family law. It turned out to be like the Public Defender's Office all over again.

I took divorce cases and worked hard to educate myself in order to give my clients the best representation. I experienced a sense of freedom as I helped people without interference from governmental bureaucracy, politicians, and judges who sometimes seemed aligned with the State.

But not everything was perfect. I entered my appearance in a dependency matter, representing a young pregnant woman. Dependency is an area of civil law in which the State of Florida petitions the court on behalf of children who are the victims of either abuse and/or neglect. In this case, my client had improperly made a 911 call during an argument with her fiancé; she stated that he had battered her. He was arrested based upon her allegations, though there was no proof of any battery.

The woman later appeared before the criminal court at her fiancé's first court date. She testified that she had lied and that there was no risk of harm. She asked the State to drop the charges, which it did. (Mind you, the soon-to-be father was in jail and had no influence on the mother's decision to drop the charges.)

Though the State dropped his criminal charges, it decided to shelter the baby when it was born because the State had determined that domestic violence *had* occurred. Essentially, the new allegations were that the mother had failed to shelter her child from the man who had battered her since she had dropped the charges against him—*even though there was no proof of the crime.*

Upon discovering that my client was in labor, I rushed to Court on Christmas morning and secured an order preventing the State from taking the child. The following week, the head prosecutor of the dependency division called me, cursing me out, saying she had scheduled a hearing, and that, if I wanted to be part of it, I had better show up for court in 20 minutes. My office was 40 minutes away. The State had engaged in an *ex parte* communication with the judge's office and had secured a hearing without coordinating the time with my office.

I arrived, just in time to watch the judge take the newborn child out of my client's arms as she nursed in order to shelter the infant in foster care.

This new area of the law was not warm and fuzzy.

Though this early experience wasn't pure family law, I realized that the best interests of children were not always considered when they undoubtedly should have been. Whatever happened to least restrictive options?! Oh, but I forgot, we challenged the government and we, including an infant, were punished.

My experience with divorce work was a little different. I had fewer negative experiences with the judges in the family law divisions, and there seemed to be a "best interest of the children" component to the statute. What I found to be challenging were the practices, behaviors, and attitudes of my opposing counsels and of the parties involved.

One interesting aspect of family law was the existence of a perfectly good process to settle cases. The issue was that cases that should have been settling were not. The attorneys and the parties were getting in the way, actually sabotaging the ability to settle.

Most of the time, the facts were not difficult, but some variables created roadblocks. Some law offices functioned around the fact that the longer the case lasted and the more work they had to do, the more money they would make. Lawyers could amp up the drama and the litigation during private conversations and instill fear in their clients. Clients acted out of emotion and spite and were easily manipulated to do what the attorneys wanted, regardless of the cost and whether they could afford it.

I FOUND COLLABORATIVE

Later that year, a good friend who had become a judge called me. She wanted me to look up something and handed me a paper with the word "collaborative" on it. I researched it and made a few calls to the number I found on the internet, but I didn't receive a return call. I continued to practice family law and to feel that something was missing. If only the parties could receive neutral input about their finances and about the needs of their children.

Years slid by and my feelings remained the same—until I found an organization called Next Generation Divorce, a new forum for collaborative professionals. More and more people were joining and attending meetings. It was exciting to hear many others expressing the same concerns I had had for years. We all wanted to help people and to provide an option that didn't require litigation.

The collaborative process leveled the imbalance of power. It created transparency and ensured that the clients' efforts and resources were focused on settling their cases in the best manner possible. It accomplished this by utilizing a team consisting of neutral professionals best suited to develop neutral options.

What a relief! For the first time, I felt that I could serve families without the interference of bullies, without the inherent conflict between the attorney and the client that drives costs and litigation, and with the ability to appropriately manage the high emotions of the spouses going through the most difficult times in their lives.

So now what?

You probably know that it can't be that easy. There must be more. And that is true. Now that we have it, where are the collaborative clients? We all realize that we still don't have the luxury to say, "Here's what we are doing now."

There are two critical variables: the opposing counsel and the opposing client. With everything that we have experienced and with every well-intentioned wish for our clients, the cases can't be collaborative unless the spouses and their attorneys agree to it.

GRASS ROOTS AND WELLBEING: MAKING THE SWITCH

Like any monumental change, this movement also requires a plan, an organized, concerted effort.

We can now help people resolve their differences in a much more constructive manner, making their lives more functional and their children stronger. This literally involves taking their conflict and turning it into peace, strength, and understanding. We address a couple's issues so that they are less likely to divorce again and so that their children's future marriages are less likely to end in divorce. This concept stands to have an enormous impact on our communities, our nation, and our world.

Divorce creates financial fallout, with a direct impact on children. People who suddenly have less are less able to be productive contributors and participants in our economy. They are less able to cope with their financial situations, such as bankruptcy and foreclosure. They have less time and are squeezed for the resources with which to raise their families. Children are caught in the arguments of their parents and the dysfunction of their parents' inability to co-parent them. Parents sabotage each other at the expense of their own children.

With so much at stake and so much to lose, who would want such hardships? What would people choose if they were presented with a custom-tailored option to help them part ways in a better manner that minimized their risk and provided strength for their children?

The grass roots effort must be there. We need the world to know that the collaborative process exists and we need people to demand it. We also need them to reject the alternative. Collaborative has to become a common phrase, to be first in the minds of people when they need it. What if couples stopped telling each other that they were going to "get a divorce" but, instead, agreed to see a collaborative professional?

People should ask their attorneys about this option. I always warn people, if you meet a lawyer who speaks negatively about collaborative, it is likely that he has not been trained or that he doesn't know how it works or what it is about. The transformation in our communities must take place on several different levels. We must work for change in the people within the communities, in the lawyers, in the judges, and in the lawmakers.

During my training as a collaborative professional, I learned about "making the switch." My switch preceded law school, during my season of discernment and self-inspection in my formative years. Essentially "the switch," in the context of collaborative training, asks an individual to relinquish his dedication to blind, zealous advocacy, void of consideration for the greater good. Through my journey, I came to realize many things: people, children, our communities, our economy, and our individual wellbeings are all important.

I think wellbeing is often overlooked. Ignoring that need is like treating the issue but never addressing the symptom. Litigation is like putting someone through intense chemotherapy with many, many side effects, but never addressing whether a less intrusive treatment could be equally or more effective. When we take care of ourselves, we are better able to see the truth and to collaborate for the wellbeing of our families, of our children, and ultimately of everyone else whom we touch.

People achieve wellbeing in many ways, from daily exercise to practicing a healthy prayer life. Paying attention to what the body needs is critical to managing stress, which then enables one to focus on making important and good decisions. My objective in seeking wellbeing is to maintain good health, to be able to be present for my friends and family in a manner that they deserve and to be the best collaborative professional that I can be.

Being a collaborative professional includes being creative and being resourceful, which are both things that I bring from my past as an artist. It means being able to find the good in people no matter what they are experiencing. I can then be a positive example and role model for people.

My transformation began with my education from the Jesuits wherein I learned the importance of mind, body, and soul and the concept of "men and women for others." I pursued and gained the ability to pull from within and to introspectively search for meaning in my actions and beliefs during my formative years in the art studio. I learned the value of creativity and the need to see the beauty in rough, uncut rock.

I looked into faces of despair and was humbled by lost and unjust odds. I was introduced to families who hurt each other through their own unmanaged devices. And I saw the light in the collaborative process to help the individual, the family, and the community at large. Lastly, I found peace in helping people and letting them know that our team could help them make it better.

I look forward to continuing my journey tomorrow. I pray for wellbeing for myself and for others, and I search for the tools to teach others how to find it. I welcome the day when I realize that the chain of dysfunction has been broken.

George Melendez is the father of two boys and the husband to his beautiful and loving wife, Kelli. He is a man who appreciates the importance of family on both a personal and a social level. His commitment to family is a theme that has woven itself throughout his career, even as far back as his time with the Office of the Guardian *ad Litem* prior to his attendance at law school. As a GAL, he serves as a volunteer advocate for children who had been abused, neglected, or abandoned, as well as privately for children embroiled in custody disputes in family law cases.

With his love for family and children, Mr. Melendez found the importance of alternative methods to resolve disputes. He is a Supreme Court certified mediator, a certified guardian *ad litem*, a parenting coordinator, and a trained collaborative professional. He prides himself on helping people understand their options, including better methods to resolve conflict, so they may focus on building and strengthening themselves and their relationships.

Mr. Melendez gained his experience as an assistant public defender, followed by his work in a small law office representing parents in family court. He has been a solo practitioner since 2010.

When out of the office, Mr. Melendez enjoys activities with his family, including baking, artwork, bike riding, and trips to the zoo.

Mr. Melendez can be reached at melendezlawoffice@me.com, or through his website, www.melendezlawoffice.com.

Litigation is unpredictable. There are so many variables that affect the outcome of a case: the disposition, mood, and history of the judge; the ability, experience, and reputation of the lawyers; the credibility, likeability, durability, intelligence, and wealth of the clients; the evidence and whether it is allowed to be admitted; the strength of the witnesses; and the length of time for the hearing and whether it is sufficient to present the desired case. These are just some of the factors that can impact a case in litigation. When considering the future of your family and life, why would anyone roll the dice in court?

The collaborative process offers those embroiled in family disputes an opportunity to choose their own fates. For clients who wish to take control of their destinies, collaborative offers them a chance to work with a team of trained professionals who consider the clients' most important goals and interests, as well as the best interests of the family as a whole, when formulating settlements.

For your family's sake, collaborate. – Ed. Note

THE COLLABORATIVE PROCESS:
RESOLVING THE PROBLEM OF RUSSIAN ROULETTE
BY JULIA BEST CHASE, ESQ.

Once upon a time, there was a paternity case involving twins. They both lived primarily with their mother, but as they got older, the son wished to live primarily with his father. The parents agreed on this, provided that the father should not have to continue paying child support to the mother.

Eventually, the son went back to living with his mother, but, not unusually, the father did not volunteer to resume paying any child support. The mother had to hire a lawyer and go to court to reinstate it.

After a grueling hearing, the judge ruled against the mother and did not order the father to pay child support. Her attorney questioned the judge's ruling by quoting the statutes and the case law that supported the mother's position, but the judge cavalierly instructed her, "Slavery was once the law. Appeal me."

This unpredictable outcome happened to my client. I was that attorney. It is not too farfetched to say that going to court can be a frustrating game of Russian Roulette.

I have been a trial lawyer for several decades. I spent the first decade as an assistant state attorney selecting jury panels to prosecute individuals who stole, hurt, or killed somebody or who were involved in something that was stolen, harmful, or could kill somebody. Enforcing the laws of the State of Florida and championing the rights of victims was both my privilege and my pleasure.

After that, I entered the family law arena and dedicated myself to helping clients cope with the traumatic death of their most intimate relationship—their marriage. After a few years of litigating, I realized that the courtroom is no place for these fragile families.

I recall with sadness a post-judgment divorce case. Before I was retained by the former wife, the two had been locked in litigation for years *after* the entry of their final judgment. The judgment ordered an equal timesharing schedule for their young son and daughter with no child support payable to the mother. At their last post-judgment mediation (there had been several), Mom felt she had been bullied into accepting no child support, and, since then, had experienced a significant decrease in income. The children, now teenagers, had increased expenses.

I explained to Mom that we could file a supplemental petition that outlined her changed financial circumstances and ask for an award of child support based upon the statutory guidelines. That sounds simple enough, right? The former husband, however, filed a supplemental counter-petition asking to modify shared parental responsibility to give him sole parental responsibility and majority timesharing. Of course, he requested that the former wife pay *him* child support.

Two years later, the guardian *ad litem* testified at trial that the daughter should spend more time with her mother because she was suffering emotionally and had even been Baker Acted. While the judge ordered child support payable to the mother, he denied *any* changes to the timesharing.

Regrettably, the daughter's reaction to this ruling was to attempt suicide while at her father's house.

Several years later, I learned that, as soon as the court closed the case, the former husband allowed Mom to exercise 100% of the overnights with their daughter and never spent time with his daughter again. Of course, he only paid the minimal child support as if he were still exercising 50% of the overnights. Mom reported being too battle fatigued and financially drained to return to court and try again.

If you are wondering if this is an unusual case, I would sadly have to answer "no." People frequently use the courtroom as a battleground. For some, it is all about winning regardless of the collateral damage. I cannot protect my clients from the overly litigious and caustic behaviors of opposing parties, nor can I prevent my client from feeling that the best course of action is responding in kind.

Many of the judges assigned to family divisions never practiced family law when they were in private practice. With so many complicated laws, rules, and issues in this field, it seems that as soon as they have a full grasp of family law, they are reassigned to another division. Some of my cases had two or three judges during their pendencies.

On top of that, it is difficult to predict an outcome due to the wide range of discretion that judges have in family law. After all, it is a court of equity. Even with perfect conditions—the parties were reasonable, the attorneys were skilled, the judges were well-versed in the law—how can a judge make the best decision about the future of two people whom she has never met based on financial affidavits and a day (or so) of listening to testimony?

The truth is—no judge can. The most qualified people to decide are the parties themselves. But, by the time a client comes to my office to discuss her case, she is often embroiled in emotionally-charged and oppositional thinking, and the lines of communication have long since broken down.

Now that I have pointed out a few of the problems with resolving matters at the courthouse, I will offer what I have found to be the best solution to the problem: the collaborative process. Contrast the earlier cases with the following scenario and decide for yourself which is the better process.

Bob was a no-nonsense, blue-collar guy in his mid-forties. He was ex-military, but you couldn't tell that from the way he melted when he talked about his kids. He often came to my office straight from work, wearing his uniform, a long-sleeved button-down light denim shirt, navy blue pants, and work boots. He wasn't exactly comfortable in a law office, but he was no stranger to them; he had consulted with other attorneys before hiring me. I asked him why he decided upon my firm.

"Because you looked me right in the eye. The other attorneys didn't look me in the eye when they spoke."

During our first consultation, I had asked him to tell me about his family.

"Beth and I have been married for ten years and have two children."

I asked, "What do you and your wife each do for a living?"

"She works part time as a nurse. I work full time as a plumber for a hospital, and I also own my own business."

"Do you own any major assets?"

"We own our home, but we owe more than it's worth."

After we went over other mundane issues, I switched gears, sensing that he was having a hard time with this divorce. "Why are you getting divorced? Do you want this?"

He was silent for a moment, first looking down at his hands, and then looking out over my shoulder. "No. I married Beth thinking that I would be married forever. We've had some issues, but what marriage doesn't?"

"So Beth is the one who initiated the divorce discussion?"

"Yes." Pain filled his eyes. "I was shocked when she told me that she wanted a divorce. I still am. I can't imagine my life without her and my children all under one roof."

Gently, I inquired, "Why do you think that she's seeking a divorce?"

"Well, like I said, our marriage isn't perfect. I guess that we do argue quite a bit."

"What do you argue about?"

"Lots of little things when we get on each other's nerves. But the big fights are about finances. She thinks I'm hiding money from her, but I'm not."

"What are your fights like?"

"They're not pretty. We raise our voices and call each other names, sometimes in front of our kids. I always regret that. Neither of us deserves that, and our kids don't need to see that. I don't want my kids to learn that type of behavior."

As he talked, Bob hung his head for a moment. "I think Beth has a problem with alcohol. I worry about who will be around to protect the kids when she passes out."

"What's your biggest fear in your divorce?"

"That I'll lose my children. She keeps threatening me that she'll get the kids if we get divorced. I'm afraid she'll move away with them. And I believe that it could happen because I've seen it happen to a buddy. I'm also afraid I'll lose my house and it's real important to me that my kids live in a house. And Beth's parents have a ton of money, so she can afford to fight it out."

This was when I had looked him in the eye. "I understand your fear, but I'll do everything I can to ensure that doesn't happen."

I saw this client headed for a contested courtroom catastrophe, so I explained the collaborative process to Bob. I suggested a team of professionals that would include a neutral mental health professional and a neutral forensic financial professional.

"The mental health professional will meet with both of you, probably both separately and together. She'll address your anger towards one another, your communication skills, and any concerns you each have about the other's parenting skills. In a similar way, the financial professional can assist in looking at your finances and ensuring that neither of you is hiding assets or income."

"That sounds great, but it sounds too expensive."

I understood. "Expense is always a concern when people get divorced. But it is cheaper to have one neutral expert rather than two dueling experts and to voluntarily produce financial documents instead of serving subpoenas and filing motions. Also, there will only be one trip to the courthouse for a five-minute uncontested final hearing instead of many trips for case management conferences, temporary relief hearings, motion hearings, mediation, and a final hearing."

"That does sound much better than the divorces I've heard about from my friends." His wisp of a smile suggested he felt a glimmer of hope.

I sent him home with a few documents explaining the collaborative process to show his wife and a website on which she could find a collaborative lawyer.

Fast-forward four months. After some individual meetings and two full team meetings, Bob, Beth, and the team attended the uncontested final hearing. As we left the courtroom, Beth asked Bob, "Would you like to go to lunch?"

I caught the eye of Beth's attorney, and we shared a smile. I had goosebumps up and down my arms, and I think the professionals, who all attended the final hearing, had the same feeling. To this day, I get a little misty retelling the story. Never, ever, have I seen two spouses exit a courtroom and act so civilly to one another, much less have one ask the other to go to lunch.

The collaborative process indeed transformed them into parents who looked ahead toward co-parenting their kids instead of ruminating on past hurts and looking for retribution. And Bob is living happily ever after in the home and sharing time with his kids.

Once upon a time there was no alternative but to "lawyer–up" and litigate, but times have changed. Family law clients can now choose the collaborative process to avoid costly and unpredictable litigation and more effectively control the outcome of their divorces.

Julia Best Chase is a family law and collaborative divorce attorney. She earned her J.D. from Touro College Jacob D. Fuchsberg Law Center in 1986 and soon thereafter was admitted to the New Jersey, New York, and Florida Bars.

After serving Hillsborough County as an assistant state attorney, Ms. Chase opened her own practice in 2000. In 2016, she became a certified volunteer guardian ad litem to oversee and protect children's interests after the Department of Children and Families has removed them from their parents due to abuse, abandonment, or neglect. Ms. Chase believes in divorce with dignity and represents clients in the collaborative divorce process.

Ms. Chase has always been extremely involved in the legal community. She has been a member of the Hillsborough County Bar Association since 1987 and has served on the collaborative section since 2013. She has also been a member of the Stann W. Givens Family Law Inn of Court since 1998, regularly serving as chair on different committees. She has been a member of the Next Generation Divorce practice group since 2015, serving as chair of the Modest Means Committee since 2016. She has been a member of the Association of Family and Conciliation Courts and the Florida Academy of Collaborative Professionals since 2016. She received the Theodore Millison Professionalism Award in 2005. She has presented on family law at countless seminars and radio presentations and has written numerous articles on the subject.

In her spare time, Ms. Chase is a Diver Master level scuba diver, having become initially NAUI certified in 1979. She loves underwater photography, creating beaded jewelry, gardening, participating in Zumba and general muscle toning, and raising backyard chickens. But her passion is raising her two children, Kinsley and John, alongside her husband, Elmer R. Chase, Jr.

Ms. Chase may be reached at jbcesquire@jbcesquire.com.

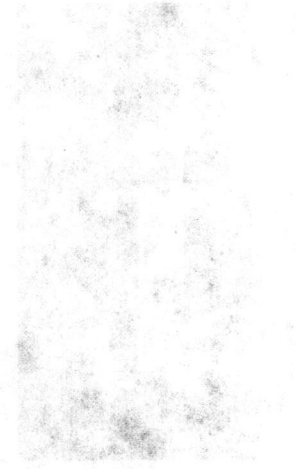

When training to become a collaborative professional, many lawyers who have only practiced in the combative, hostile setting of litigation are uncertain if they will be able to make the all-important paradigm shift. Can a bulldog litigator who only knows the courtroom switch gears and become a peacemaker? Should a team bother to invite a professional onto a collaborative team who has that aggressive reputation?

Many seasoned litigators are not cut out for collaboration. They do not understand how to zealously advocate for a client without constantly reminding her of what could happen in court or threatening the other spouse to go to court. They do not comprehend that a resolution can be met without acting positionally. They can't let go of the idea that they should be fighting for their client to "win" and for the other client to "lose."

But many former litigators embrace the collaborative model, after having seen firsthand the destruction caused to families by litigation. They turn out to be some of the better collaborators because they understand that the alternative approach destroys families and is unhealthy for the clients and the professionals. So, if you can teach a former litigator new tricks, you should! – Ed. Note

YOU *CAN* TEACH A FORMER LITIGATOR NEW TRICKS
BY REBECCA A. GRAHAM, ESQ. AND GALE MOORE, ESQ.

While collaboration seems like the opposite of litigation, some of the traits that make a good litigator can also make a successful collaborating attorney. For example, both must be honest and put their clients' needs above their own need to "win."

The following story about a collaborative divorce is told from the perspective of both clients' attorneys. One had been trained in collaborative practice, but the other had not yet. Still, they had litigated against each other in the past, and each had impressed the other with her ability to focus both on how to achieve her client's goals while still satisfying those of her client's spouse and also on the best interests of the entire family.

REBECCA GRAHAM, COLLABORATIVE ATTORNEY FOR HUSBAND

Sam came to me seeking a divorce from his wife, Carol. For our initial consultation, he was formal and business-like, dressed in slacks, a collared shirt, and a tie. He was in his fifties, with graying hair at his temples and laugh lines around his eyes and mouth.

I tried to make him as comfortable as possible. "Tell me a bit about yourself."

He uncrossed his legs and leaned forward while he nervously clicked a pen. "I married my college sweetheart, Carol, right after we finished grad school. Although we both went to the same college and have similar degrees, since we've been married, I've been the major income earner and financial decision-maker. That was okay with me because Carol raised our children, and she did a wonderful job. But we've lived more like siblings than marriage partners for almost 20 years. Since the kids have gone to college, it's time for me to finally be happy."

"I see. Does Carol know that you want a divorce?"

"We've discussed the possibility throughout our marriage, so it shouldn't come as too much of a shock to her, but she doesn't know that I'm talking to you today."

"How do you think that she'll take the news?"

"Honestly, I think she'll be devastated. I don't want to upset her, but I see no other choice. I want to be happy." He crossed and uncrossed his legs, all while staring at the wall behind me. Finally, he said quietly, "I've met someone else. I'm not proud of it, but I can't help myself. She makes me feel like a teenager again, happy and in love. I want that feeling in my life. I deserve that." He looked at me.

"I understand." I held his gaze and paused. "Does Carol know that you've met someone?"

Sam shook his head and lowered his head into his hands. "I don't think so. I know that it's horrible to think this way, but I've worked so hard, and we have so much now, but I'm afraid that she's going to get it all. I've done a lot of research, and I know that Florida is a no-fault state. But I'm concerned that, due to the length of our marriage and my infidelity, we could end up in angry and expensive litigation. I've seen it happen to too many of my friends."

I encouraged him. "It doesn't have to be that way, though. Let me explain your options."

After we discussed his choices, he sounded more confident than he had during our entire hour together. "Collaborative divorce, that's what I want. And I think Carol will too, once she understands our choices."

"I think that it's your best option. When will you talk to her about this?"

"Tonight. I have to. I can't wait any longer."

"I'll give you a list of attorneys that you can give her so she can decide if she wants to choose collaborative. I'll point out a few people I've worked with before and who I know are wonderful attorneys."

"Thank you. This is going to be really hard, but I feel so much better after talking with you."

GALE MOORE, COLLABORATIVE ATTORNEY FOR WIFE

Mine was one of the names on the list Rebecca had given Sam to give to his wife. The morning Carol came into my office she was searching for answers. She was dressed somewhat matronly in Ann Taylor khakis and a shirt buttoned to the top. I could tell she had once been pretty, but she now had bags under her eyes and wrinkles around her mouth.

She began stoically, "I've accepted that the man I've been married to for 20 years no longer wants to be with me, but I don't really know what that means for me. I've always relied on his income and financial guidance. We met in graduate school. Even though I have a degree similar to Sam's, he's always been the primary breadwinner."

"Did you stay at home to raise your children?"

"Yes. That was always our plan. We are both very traditional in that sense, but now our two children are in college."

"What was your marriage like? Were you happy?"

Carol thought for a moment. "I was content. Throughout our marriage, Sam struggled to stay faithful, which was very difficult for me. It was hard to trust him. I understand that he's involved with another woman now, and I think that's why he wants out, but I don't see why this affair is any different from the others."

"Any idea why he had such a hard time with fidelity?"

She cringed a bit. "He had some issues from his childhood, watching his father cheat on his mother, and I don't think that he ever really dealt with it. Before we were married, he always said he'd never do that to me, but it was always a problem. He needs counseling, but he told me he's following through with individual therapy." She shrugged. "It's a decision only he can make."

"What's your biggest concern in your divorce?"

She took off her glasses and rubbed her eyes. "I'd like our divorce to be amicable, but I'm concerned about my future. I've always allowed, in fact, encouraged Sam to make our money-related decisions. And now that our marriage is over, I have to face the fact that I know little about our finances. I've completely relied on him all these years to take care of that. I want to be sure I understand our finances and can handle my own after the divorce. I have no idea what assets and liabilities we have or how it all works. Now, I'm not sure I can trust him in light of his infidelity, but I'm hoping for the best."

A collaborative approach could be a good option for her, given her willingness and desire to maintain an amicable relationship with her husband and to learn as much about her finances as possible. I explained the divorce process options and was happy when she emphatically chose, "Collaborative. That's the option Sam mentioned, and I understand why he felt it was our best choice."

Once she left, I contacted Sam's lawyer. "Rebecca, I just met with Carol, and she seems on board for collaborative and thought her husband was, as well. How would you like to proceed?"

"I got that impression from him, too. Let's set up a meeting with the four of us to discuss this in greater depth."

I projected a calm demeanor during the meeting at which we had an open and forthright discussion with Carol and Sam about their futures. Like the process in general, this first meeting was a combination of patience, transparency, and thought-provoking questions.

REBECCA GRAHAM, COLLABORATIVE ATTORNEY FOR HUSBAND

I was pleased when Gale contacted me, saying Carol had retained her and that she wanted to explore a collaborative divorce. Gale and I had been on opposing sides in the past. Years ago, we had litigated a very nasty child custody case. During that difficult case, though we disagreed on facts and legal positions, I respected her and came to know her as honest and ethical. Consequently, I was optimistic about collaborative success for Sam and Carol.

As we expected and as is common in almost every dissolution process, one spouse, in this case, Sam, was mostly responsible for gathering financial documents. The financial professional relied on him to produce additional information throughout the process.

Carol often had questions about the nature, veracity, or extent of the information he provided. In order to satisfy her concerns, Gale requested additional investigation and analysis, but without suggesting that Sam had handled financial matters in a dishonest or secretive manner. Consequently, rather than becoming indignant or encouraging my client to feel that his credibility was being questioned, I was in a good position to encourage Sam to cooperate. In addition, I could urge him to be patient while Gale and Carol, who was less comfortable with finances, digested the information.

A collaborative process does not mean that there are no disagreements or tense moments. Although Sam may have been considered the offending spouse, it was also true that he had worked hard for the sake of the family and deserved a secure financial future, as did Carol. It was important for me to make sure that Sam did not concede too much out of any guilt he felt.

I am sure Gale felt defensive or protective about certain issues relating to Carol as well. Both Gale and I made an effort to check our aggressive natures at the door and allow the financial and mental health experts to keep us on track with problem-solving. As a result, we used our time wisely, rather than for posturing.

At one point, Carol took a strong position about her desire that Sam should pay for the adult children's postgraduate education. Even though she would not have prevailed in court on that issue, her concerns about it were blocking our way to settlement because it was what was most important to her.

Sam did not want to be required to pay for postgraduate education; he wanted to do it of his own volition. Ultimately, our constructive working relationship led the team to devise a settlement that would not legally obligate my client and would enable Carol to use her own post-dissolution assets to support the children through graduate school. I doubt she will have to bear that expense alone, but knowing that she could smoothed the path to resolution.

On another occasion, Gale and I had an opportunity to diffuse a misunderstanding between the clients about alimony that had almost caused a complete breakdown of the collaborative process. Once again, we did not necessarily agree with the other client's viewpoints, but, because we could discuss issues in a respectful manner, we were able to come up with ways to guide our clients to compromise.

GALE MOORE, COLLABORATIVE ATTORNEY FOR WIFE

We resolved the matter in a matter of months. The collaborative approach allowed Carol the benefit of a financial neutral to help gather and organize all of their financial information. This also minimized their costs because they did not need to hire two battling financial experts, as they would have done if they had litigated. During the process, it became clear that after the divorce Carol would need some further assistance to plan her financial future, so the team referred her to a financial planner. Sam could have been threatened by this, but Rebecca knew this was going to happen and why it was important. She was able to explain it to him so that he understood the importance of it. That insight allowed the matter to move forward unhampered.

One of the biggest benefits of the collaborative approach to me was the use of the mental health facilitator. She helped all of the professionals understand the interpersonal dynamics between the clients, including their backgrounds and perceptions, which enabled all of us to do our best for them. As the matter wrapped up, the mental health facilitator pointed out that she believed the relationship between the lawyers had been one of the primary reasons the collaboration had moved forward so smoothly and effectively.

I have known Rebecca for years and have known her to be a zealous advocate for her clients. She is thorough, professional, and straightforward. We were able to work well with one another and the rest of the team to help these clients find resolution, while Rebecca and I each strove individually to achieve the best result for our clients.

REBECCA GRAHAM, COLLABORATIVE ATTORNEY FOR HUSBAND

The collaborative process takes some getting used to for attorneys who have litigated most or all of their professional lives. Sitting around a table with five people for hours, mostly listening, seems foreign to someone who is used to conducting depositions, cross-examining, and making arguments to the court. An advocate's ability to put her own ego aside in exchange for an overall optimal result has a contagious effect. A lawyer's ability to respect and trust the other spouse's attorney allows the clients to respect and trust each other and thus paves the way for a successful outcome.

Clients expect their lawyers to guide them, which means that they also look to their lawyers to show them how to behave. I am proud that my professional relationship with Gale encouraged our clients to exercise patience, restraint, and trust that ultimately led to a resolution of all of their issues in just a few months' time.

A successful collaboration is professionally rewarding. It is gratifying to see clients and their children experience as little trauma and ongoing conflict as possible. It gives clients a feeling of power and control over their lives. It provides the attorney with the satisfaction of knowing that all of that can be accomplished while still protecting her client's rights and interests.

Rebecca A. Graham has practiced marital and family law in Clearwater and Tampa Bay, Florida, for 20 years. Although she is a native of Tampa, she received her B.A. from Texas A&M University and her law degree at Texas Tech.

Ms. Graham is a member of the Florida Bar family law section. She was elected to the board of directors for the Clearwater Bar Association in 2016 and is a former chair of the family law section of the Clearwater Bar Association.

Although she has handled over 50 family law related trials, she has been practicing in the collaborative field for over ten years and hopes to continue to focus on the growth of collaborative practice.

Ms. Graham became actively interested in collaborative when the Tampa Bay legal community began organizing and training collective practitioners. She recently received advanced training and hopes to continue to increase her practice in this area. She is a member of the newly-formed collaborative section of the Clearwater Bar Association.

Ms. Graham is married and has two adult children. She is an avid hockey fan and enjoys the outdoors and travel in her spare time.

Ms. Graham may be reached at Office@RGrahamLaw.com.

Gale Moore is a board-certified attorney in marital and family law. Ms. Moore received her B.A. from the University of North Carolina at Chapel Hill and her J.D. from Stetson Law School. She has over two decades of courtroom experience, having served as an assistant public defender early in her career until she opened her own law practice in the late 90s. Since then, she has focused on family law with an emphasis on amicable resolution of matters whenever possible.

She is certified by the Florida Supreme Court as a family law mediator and has served as a court-appointed guardian *ad litem* in high-conflict family law cases since the inception of such appointments in Pinellas County.

Ms. Moore has served on the board of directors of the Clearwater Bar Association, as chair of the family law section of the Clearwater Bar Association, and currently, as co-chair of the newly-formed collaborative law section of the Clearwater Bar Association. She has served on the executive board of the Canakaris Family Law Inn of Court, as well as secretary liaison to the American Inn. She is presently serving as executive director-elect of the American Inn. In 2015, Ms. Moore received the John C. Lenderman Award for Excellence in Family Law for her exemplary contributions to the family law profession by the Canakaris Inn of Court.

You may reach Ms. Moore at Gale@GaleHMoore.com.

Just because a professional is competent, likeable, and successful does not mean that he will make a good collaborative teammate. There are certain qualities that all successful collaborative professionals share. When one quality is missing in any of the team members, the entire team will suffer and the chance of the clients reaching a successful resolution will be diminished.

Having "social smarts" is the ability to interact and communicate appropriately with those around you, understand social cues, and understand what others are thinking and how they are feeling. Personal humility is the ability to be humble and courteously respectful to others. Professional will is the ability to be friendly, helpful, and cooperative in a professional setting.

When all members of a collaborative team show these three virtues, even the most difficult issues can be resolved, and collaborative magic can happen. If you are lacking in one of these virtues, there is still hope. If you have a strong desire to be a collaborative success and if you are cognizant of these virtues and on which ones you must especially make a conscious effort, you can be a collaborative superstar. – Ed. Note

THE THREE VIRTUES
OF A HIGHLY EFFECTIVE COLLABORATIVE TEAM MEMBER
BY J. DAVID HARPER, CPA, ABV, PFS, CFF, CBA, CVA

There are moments in collaborative matters when all progress halts. Clients seem unable to move beyond apparently minor issues. They become increasingly positional, revisit the same issues repeatedly, or blame the professionals for the lack of progress. At times like these, the team feels like they've lost control of the process. They can become paralyzed, causing the process to run far longer than expected and to degenerate into offer/counter-offer scenarios, or ultimately, an impasse.

Yet, great teams push through those moments for a successful outcome. Some outstanding teams even know how to avoid those progress-halting moments entirely.

What are the common threads of a highly effective team? We will explore why a successful collaborative matter often has little to do with the professional team's set of specialized qualifications or technical expertise. In fact, a purely *academic* skill set can often impede real progress. Instead, success may have far more to do with a specific set of virtues shared by all of the team members. When one or more of these three virtues are absent, the matter is likely to lose momentum or even fall apart; when all three virtues are present, the stage is set for magical moments and good results.

So, what are these virtues?

SOCIAL SMARTS

The veins in the neck of the emotionally-charged spouse were bulging. He slid his own CPA's business valuation across the conference room table at me to prove how "wrong" my valuation was. As the financial neutral, I do not always agree to perform the business valuation for the collaborative team. Often, the team brings in another professional for that so that the perception of my neutrality remains intact.

However, the family finances were tight, and they needed a valuation completed "yesterday," so I agreed. Needless to say, Bill was not a fan of my numbers and demanded that I either adjust the value or explain why his CPA's numbers were wrong. His threatening demeanor was particularly offensive given the high-stress "hoop-jumping" we encountered to deliver an accurate and well-articulated report at record pace. I briefly glanced down at the spreadsheets slid in front of me and considered my response.

In these moments, it's difficult for left-brained "bean counters" married to numbers and facts to shift to the art of clear communication with two often highly emotional clients during one of their most stressful seasons of life.

What do accountants do? Accountants *count*, right? We chose a profession that only deals with numbers (or so we thought).

Growing up, we enjoyed solving formulas over social interaction. We sailed through statistics and struggled through Shakespeare. As high school seniors, we wore T-shirts to school on math test days that read "AP Calculus" on the front and "What's Your Problem?" on the back. (Or maybe that was just me.) We are a different breed. Yet, we financial folks, and all of us as collaborative professionals, find ourselves in an environment in which the "art" of social interaction and clear communication cannot be more crucial to our work.

I responded incorrectly. I viewed his tough words as a binary choice: either I (1) adjust the value or (2) prove why his CPA was wrong. When I chose door number 2, quickly dismissing his CPA's work, I failed to see the other factors at play.

After a brief break and some wise counsel from our facilitator (mental health professional), I re-entered the room and led a discussion that should have taken place initially, essentially a "do-over."

First, we considered other options. We could include his CPA's valuation for the team to consider. We could contact another top professional in the community for feedback. Or the wife could get her own independent valuation and we could average the values. And a fourth option was to consider an offset to his valuation with other items on the equitable distribution schedule or support calculations. The solutions were plentiful.

Then, we addressed the emotion embedded in his words. Behind his hostile tone were deep insecurities and the need to be heard and understood. We acknowledged his real concerns over the uncertainty of his business and future outlook in general. We validated the difficult family and financial decisions he faced. We stressed to him that we truly had his and his family's best interest at heart and would do whatever it took to help them through this season of life. Finally, he began to soften.

Even though it was a difficult matter, ultimately, they accepted our original valuation and made it successfully through the collaborative process. However, without the wise guidance of our facilitator and social smarts of our attorneys, the matter would have almost certainly resulted in impasse.

Our success had very little to do with the actual value we placed on the business but almost everything to do with *how* the professional team addressed the couple's emotions, concerns, and goals.

Highly effective collaborative professionals understand that the process breaks down more often from a lack of social smarts and effective listening, understanding, and responding than it does from shortfalls in technical or legal expertise.

Effective team members hear the meaning behind the words spoken. They know when to empathize with their client through a simple facial expression or momentary pause. They also know when to push back on their client or quash a negative statement regarding other team members, keeping them focused forward.

Great collaborative professionals also know how to watch for signs of *foul play* by one of the clients. Sometimes one will make a comment such as, "He's hiding funds and you've got to find it!" If this is repeated (often in a loud, angry voice), but there are no indications of dishonest activity, it could be a red flag for the spouse making the accusation.

Guilt often accompanies those who shout the loudest. Distrust and anger toward the other spouse sometimes come from guilt. This played out in a divorce in which, a year after the matter resolved, the accusing spouse was found to have undisclosed accounts.

Another sign of potential foul play is a response that doesn't seem to match the question. In a recent matter, the husband told me privately that the wife had a safety deposit box with over $100,000 in cash in it. When I questioned her separately, she said abruptly, "No. Why do you keep asking me about that? Are you working for him?!" It was the *first* time I had asked her, but clearly, my question elicited instant defensiveness. She responded by deflecting and making accusations.

Highly effective collaborative professionals hear what is unsaid. They "live in the question" with their clients. They know there is a better alternative than to begin a sentence with "I think" or "I suggest" and understand it is often far more effective to frame any thoughts as questions: "Do you think it would be helpful to…?" They know how to place open-ended questions back on the spouses, such as: "What options have you thought of?" They understand that these questions help to empower the clients and remind them that this is their choice and their outcome.

PERSONAL HUMILITY

In his book, *Good to Great*, Jim Collins explores why some companies become great companies while others do not. Collins and his research team note the common characteristics of these elite companies scattered throughout the world and how they were able to leap to greatness, outperforming their peers for decades.

Collins asks, "What type of leadership was required to achieve greatness?" Shockingly, the larger-than-life, egocentric CEOs with big personalities (in other words, the *smartest guys* in the room) consistently belonged to those companies who *failed* to achieve great results. By contrast, the CEOs of the elite companies with sustained great results possessed a different pattern of leadership: *humility*. Collins and his research team were shocked to find that those who worked with or wrote about the leaders of these elite companies continually described them as "quiet, humble, modest, reserved, shy, gracious, mild-mannered, self-effacing, understated."

The leaders of these elite companies also avoided talking about themselves. During interviews, they would talk about "[t]he company and the contributions of other executives . . . but would deflect discussion about their own contributions." According to Collins and his research team, the top leaders of these great companies never aspired to be put on a pedestal or become larger-than-life heroes or unreachable icons. As Collins describes them, "They were seemingly ordinary people quietly producing extraordinary results."

Some confuse humility with a lack of self-confidence, but the opposite is usually true. The most confident professionals I know and with whom I work are also the humblest. These people no longer feel the need to prove their worth or seem to care about casting themselves in the most positive light. They dive into the team's needs and, as Collins mentions, quietly produce extraordinary results for the good of the team. Their focus is not on themselves, but on others. As author C.S. Lewis explains, "Humility isn't thinking less of yourself, but thinking of yourself less."

When I start to care more about my client's perceptions of me than I do about their interests and what needs to be accomplished, I'm in trouble. Humility is found in abandoning "self" (self-

49

centeredness, self-interests, self-preservation) to be solely concerned with the clients' interests and the needs of the team. Ego is contagious. Fortunately, so is humility. How does humility spread? Humility spreads as team members *praise* (others) and *seek constructive criticism* (of themselves).

PROFESSIONAL WILL

The year was 1912 and Theodore Roosevelt was campaigning for re-election. By the evening of October 14, his campaign had carried him to Milwaukee, Wisconsin, where he was to deliver a speech in the city's public auditorium. As he was leaving his hotel to be driven there, a saloonkeeper named John Shrank approached him with his pistol and fired a bullet into Roosevelt's chest, knocking him down. As bystanders subdued the gunman, Roosevelt stood up and surveyed his blood-spattered shirt and bullet wound. He then forced himself to cough, as he had learned from his army days, to see if he was coughing blood due to significant internal bleeding. Finding no blood in his saliva, he demanded that he be driven to the auditorium to deliver his speech.

The bullet had penetrated a copy of the speech notes he was carrying in his jacket, which had slowed the bullet down enough to save his life. His doctors later found the bullet lodged between two of his ribs, half an inch from his lung, and decided it too dangerous to attempt to remove, so Roosevelt carried it in his chest until his death in 1919.

That night of October 14, Roosevelt convinced the entourage accompanying him on the sidewalk that his message and the "matters at hand" far exceeded the significance of his own life. He travelled to the auditorium and stood at the podium, to the crowd's utter shock and disbelief. Still wearing his torn and red-stained shirt, he pulled out his blood-spattered notes and began his speech, "I have a message to deliver, and I will deliver it as long as there is life in my body." His speech lasted for nearly an hour before he retired to the hospital for treatment.

While none of us as collaborative professionals will have to face something so dramatic, Roosevelt's example is a challenge to all of us to live a life engaged in a vision bigger than ourselves, a life in which the *message* is more important than the *messenger*. When those moments arise when progress halts and the team is seemingly unable to move the clients beyond positional or emotional issues, it is tempting for us to passively disengage and shift our attention onto other, easier matters we feel are more productive.

It is also tempting, if we also have litigation clients, to spend countless hours preparing for court, but only a few moments preparing for collaborative meetings. After all, there's no judge, no "real" deadlines, and often little formality. Highly effective team members maintain a *professional will* that, regardless of the circumstances, they never break from the discipline of attentiveness and preparation. They set clear deadlines and hold themselves and the clients accountable for what needs to be done.

Preparing for collaborative meetings may be even more important than preparing for court. In court, you are delivering the facts to the judge. In collaborative, you are communicating the same set of facts often to both the CEO and the stay-at-home spouse, to both the financially illiterate and the savvy, and managing the team's dynamics as you go. Collaborative requires preparation for both presenting the facts and the art of doing so in an understanding and option-building way.

While we set a professional environment for these meetings, we also create a comfortable one. "Appropriate humor" was the term used by a recent client at the conclusion of his collaborative matter to describe the healthy environment the team established during full team meetings. It led to better option building and creative thinking. Highly effective professionals are so prepared for meetings that they come across as spontaneous, flexible, creative, and, at times, they use appropriate humor.

As the financial neutral, I normally have the details of my plan for the meeting on my laptop in front of me—usually in Word documents and Excel spreadsheets—yet I rarely need to share all of this information during the full team meeting. I generally begin my comments seated at the table, and then, after a brief explanation, move to the white board to facilitate conversation. I have all the material I need, but I focus our attention on the single discussion topic.

Professional will requires a dedication to urgency. In our

collaborative matters, we are often "walking up a downward moving escalator." Money continues flowing in and out of accounts, and the couple and their children continue along their emotional roller coasters. The team must be dedicated to maintaining forward momentum by keeping clear expectations and deadlines. As author Patrick Lencioni states, "Ambiguity is the enemy of accountability."

TEAM ASSESSMENT

When a matter loses momentum, the professional team should ask themselves, "Is one of these three virtues missing?"

When a team member has personal humility and professional will but lacks social smarts, he does not understand how the others receive his words and actions. The good news is that this "guilty" team member does not have bad intentions. Normally, with the help of other team members, this person can quickly and humbly accept the corrective feedback and clean up the communication issues.

When a team member has personal humility and social smarts but lacks professional will, everyone loves him because he is humble, empathetic, and good at caring for the needs of other team members; however, he tends to do only as much as he is asked and is rarely proactive in keeping other team members accountable. This can dramatically reduce team efficiency and prolong the time it takes to complete the matter.

When a team member has social smarts and professional will but lacks personal humility, he is socially persuasive and works hard, but only as much as will benefit him personally. This type is particularly dangerous because he is rooted in personal self-interest. These people are often difficult to detect as they are skilled at appearing humble. A lack of humility (or ego) is also difficult to identify within ourselves. Team members who lack humility often refuse to admit their mistakes and struggle to be vulnerable with others. The result is often a lack of trust; and, as we all know, once trust is lost, it is difficult to recover.

Highly effective teams are committed to continual self-improvement and embrace the virtues of social smarts, personal humility, and professional will. As collaborative professionals, we all share a special passion. It extends well beyond financial gain, professional accolades, and personal recognition. It's a shared belief that how we conduct our matters can actually make a positive difference in people's lives—that through collaborative practice, we are building a better way for families to overcome crisis. But it's often hard to see what difference we can make on a larger scale. Robert F. Kennedy said:

> Let no one be discouraged by the belief there is nothing one man [or one woman] can do against the enormous array of the world's ills .... Few will have the greatness to bend history itself; but each of us can work to change a small portion of events, and in the total of all those acts will be written the history of this generation . . . . It is from the numberless diverse acts of courage and belief that human history is shaped. Each time a man [or woman] stands up for an ideal, or acts to improve the lot of others, . . . he [or she] sends a tiny ripple of hope, and crossing each other from a million different centers of energy, those ripples build a current which can sweep down the mightiest walls of oppression and resistance.

May we, as collaborative professionals, use our social smarts, personal humility, and professional will to send tiny ripples of hope to families throughout our communities and to embrace the belief that, together, through our collaborative practices, we can redefine the current that carries us through crisis for generations to come.

J. David Harper, CPA, ABV, PFS, CFF, CBA, CVA has extensive experience serving as the financial neutral in collaborative divorce matters and is a leading member of both collaborative divorce professional organizations in Tampa, Florida. He has written and presented on a wide range of topics, including collaborative practice, family law financial procedures, business valuation, and forensic accounting.

Mr. Harper specializes in business valuation, forensic accounting, and litigation support services, serving as financial neutral, expert witness, joint expert, and court-appointed expert.

Mr. Harper holds a master's degree in accounting from the University of Virginia. Prior to that, he graduated *summa cum laude* from Auburn University with a bachelor's degree in international business with a finance concentration. He is a certified public accountant in Florida and Georgia. In addition to his CPA designations, Mr. Harper is also accredited in business valuation (ABV), a personal financial specialist (PFS), and certified in financial forensics (CFF) through the American Institute of Certified Public Accountants. He is also a certified business appraiser (CBA) through the Institute of Business Appraisers and a certified valuation analyst (CVA) through the National Association of Certified Valuators and Analysts. Mr. Harper has completed numerous advanced trainings in the collaborative divorce process. His past experience and training as an investment advisor representative and general securities representative (Series 7 and Series 66 licensed) through the Financial Industry Regulatory Authority enable him to better serve his clients in a neutral capacity.

He and his wife, Laurie, are the proud parents of four children. You may reach Mr. Harper at DHarper@TampaForensic.com.

Collaborative magic can sometimes be seen during the lighter moments of meetings. Although the collaborative team respects the serious nature of helping a couple dissolve their marriage, when appropriate and respectfully delivered, humor can provide a much-needed release of stress for the couple and the professionals. This is just another one of the many benefits of collaborative. Hardly do you find humor during court proceedings. But many collaborative clients and professionals become so close and comfortable with those on their teams that laughter can be heard frequently coming from the conference room. This natural stress reliever can help teams think more creatively about possible resolutions and can help clients feel more secure in making important, life-changing decisions. – Ed. Note

WHEN LAUGHTER FILLS THE ROOM
BY ADAM B. CORDOVER, ESQ.

When families undergo a traditional courtroom divorce, often the only laughter you hear is spiteful, aimed like a weapon to cut down or to mock the other person. People use bullying laughter to deflect attention away from their own faults.

And yet, a different type of laughter can sometimes be heard in meetings for a collaborative divorce—the kind that embraces the good times that the spouses had. It accompanies recollections of adorable firsts of the children and acknowledges inside jokes those restructuring their family share.

I was recently in a full team collaborative meeting in a conference room at a Tampa law firm. I represented the husband, Eli, a successful businessman in his late forties who had a penchant for bowties and suspenders and who often ran his fingers up and down his suspenders when he was listening, nervous, or angry.

Because it was a full team meeting, the neutral facilitator, neutral financial professional, Eli's wife, and her attorney were also present. Eli's wife, Margo, was a pretty but somewhat reserved woman who always wore vibrant blouses over conservative slacks. Every comment she made, even the most mundane, sounded like criticism or nagging to her husband.

We were debating some tough issues and were about to discuss how the family's assets and debts would be divided. You could feel that the nerves in the room were heightened and that Eli and Margo were both on edge.

And that's when I said it. "Okay, now it is time to talk about E.D.," referring, of course, to the lawyer's shorthand for "equitable distribution," or allocating the couple's assets and liabilities.

The clients instantly shot each other a raised eyebrow and then cracked up. At first, I wasn't sure what was going on, but when the neutral facilitator began giggling, I realized what they thought I was referring to, which sent the rest of the table into a fit of laughter.

Eli quipped, while running his fingers up and down his suspenders, "Of all the problems in our marriage, E.D. was not one of them."

His comment brought everyone to hysterics and was a much-needed icebreaker before we returned to our difficult conversation. Once everyone regained their composure, notable relief filled the room, and the entire team grew more relaxed. The emotional shift enabled us to craft a creative agreement that met both spouses' most important goals and interests.

We had other moments of laughter. While discussing the parenting plan and whether Eli would be able to get their daughter to her after-school activities on time after work on his days with her, Margo showed the team a picture of their daughter in her ballet tutu at age 5. Everyone "oohed and awed" over how adorable she was.

The team facilitator asked, "So is she still in dance? I don't recall either of you mentioning that activity."

Eli's eyes crinkled as he met Margo's, fondly saying, "That was some recital, wasn't it?"

Margo responded with laughter. "Samantha looked adorable in her tutu, but she was a terrible dancer! She kept going the opposite way of the other dancers, and when she didn't know what to do, she would just twirl around in circles."

Chuckling, Eli continued, "She finally sat down on the stage to play with the pink ribbon in her hair and didn't get up until the end of the production. I think she forgot she was on stage. The other kids danced around her like she wasn't there!"

Margo finished, "That was her first and last dance recital!" We all chuckled at the thought of their daughter's unique performance.

Discussions of parenting plans are often highly sensitive subjects, so the charming story helped to ease the mood in the room and allowed them to talk seriously about her best interests.

At another point in the meeting, while finalizing their marital settlement agreement, they fell into their apparently age-old spirited debate of whether periwinkle was a shade of purple or a shade of blue. As the facilitator handed out pens to sign the agreement, Margo began their joke, holding up a blueish pen, and saying with a wink, "Eli, doesn't this pen write in the prettiest shade of periwinkle?"

Eli laughed, "Margo, you're blind. That pen is blue. Everyone knows that periwinkle is a shade of purple."

Margo continued, mocking offense, "It is not. It is a shade of blue. That's a fact. Look it up." She looked to the rest of the team to back her up."

Coincidentally, I agreed with Margo. "It is a shade of blue," I added, somewhat apologetically. "Of course, I'm a bit colorblind."

Margo's attorney piped up, "No, Eli's right, it's a shade of purple."

This debate continued until the financial professional used his smartphone, "According to Webster's Dictionary, periwinkle is a shade of lavender, which everyone knows is a pale purple."

Eli stood, put his hands in the air like a champion, and pranced a victory lap around the conference table. "Finally! We've been arguing about this for almost 20 years!"

As Eli celebrated, Margo giggled, and threw wadded up paper at him, saying, "I'll never admit defeat! Periwinkle *is* a shade of blue. I just know it. I don't care what the dictionary says!"

Eli sat back at the table and looked Margo in the eye. "Ok. You and I are going to have to be on the same page with our kids, even if at times we disagree. And so, in that spirit, I say let's throw the dictionary definition out, and agree to put in the agreement that periwinkle is, despite what anyone else says, a shade of blue. Deal?"

"Deal!" Margo happily concluded.

This fun exchange helped to lighten the seriousness of the process. In their final divorce documents, a handwritten clause proclaimed an agreement on the color of periwinkle. Eli and Margo left that final meeting smiling.

More than once, an attorney with the law firm at which we met, whose office was across from our conference room, poked her head in and asked us to quiet down, as she was meeting with a client in her office.

The shushing attorney, a friend of mine, told me later that her client was suffering through a conventional courtroom divorce. The client wondered why there was so much laughter in the conference room. When told that people were settling their issues collaboratively, the client exclaimed, "You mean to tell me that they are going through a divorce and they're laughing together?!"

While laughter crops up in the collaborative process, it is rare in traditional litigation—yet another reason why collaborative practice is healthier for families.

Laughter and humor, when used appropriately, helps. Why?

1. It establishes intimacy and creates bonds between team members. It unites people and makes them more likeable. Laughter triggers an automatic response in the listener's brain that helps us to interact socially by priming us to smile, laugh, and connect with others. If we can all laugh together, then we must not be all that different.
2. It creates a level playing field, especially for clients who are intimidated by all the professionals. When a professional cracks a few appropriate jokes, it humanizes him. It reduces the social distance between professionals and clients.
3. Laughter is a great equalizer that facilitates conversation and builds trust.
4. Those who use humor well are typically viewed as more credible, prepared, and in control.
5. Laughter makes difficult conversations easier because it introduces an element of levity.

6. It offers a different perspective, sometimes allowing people to see that they are being unrealistic or unfair in their desires. Respectfully showing the absurdity of a position can get a client back on track.
7. It makes people want to listen to what you have to say and more likely to remember what you have said.
8. Humor promotes active listening because it distracts people from immediately creating counter arguments.
9. Humor allows for better decision-making because those experiencing good moods are more flexible, as well as able to think unconventionally and analytically.
10. The hormone released from laughter, serotonin, improves focus and objectivity. Laughter also decreases stress hormones and triggers the release of endorphins, the body's natural feel-good chemical that promotes an overall sense of wellbeing and diminishes pain. And those who feel good negotiate more reasonably.
11. Laughter stimulates the entire body. So, teams that are beginning to drag after long negotiations will feel energized and refreshed after sharing a good laugh. It boosts your oxygen intake, causing you to feel more awake.
12. Humor increases motivation and productivity, which in a collaborative divorce means that matters will be resolved more quickly and less expensively.
13. It can turn a tense moment into a fresh, relaxed space in which to negotiate. It often provides a much-needed release during stressful negotiations. Laughter diffuses anger and conflict and helps people to move on to more important, productive conversations.
14. It gives people hope because, if they are able to laugh during these hard moments, maybe things aren't all bad.

In the divorce above, Eli and Margo initiated the humor (except, of course, for the first incident when I did so inadvertently), but there are appropriate ways for professionals to inject humor into full team meetings. Follow these tips to decide if a little humor would benefit your collaborative team:

1. Know your audience. If either spouse is too upset or emotional to appreciate your humor, don't use it.
2. Be respectful. Don't use humor to make fun of a client or a professional. Laugh *with* people, not *at* people.
3. Avoid making light of a serious situation or dismissing a client's valid concerns.
4. Apply humor to situations, rather than to people.
5. You may know your professional team well enough to have inside jokes with one another. They aren't appropriate if you don't share the meaning of them with the clients.
6. Make light of yourself. If you model not taking yourself so seriously, the team should follow suit.
7. Don't direct all "humor" toward one person, even if he appears to be taking it well. Remember that you are creating a team environment, not an "us versus them" mentality.
8. Know when to quit. If your attempt at humor is not going over well, just stop. You don't want to appear as though you don't respect the clients' feelings and the major trauma that they are experiencing.
9. Only use humor at appropriate times. Don't use it in a way that makes people feel left out or singled out. Avoid creating a situation in which a client feels like she doesn't understand something that was said or what was meant. Use humor to make people more comfortable, not more awkward.
10. Be imaginative. Creatively re-framing words in a humorous way can show a person a different perspective.
11. Always avoid discriminatory humor that could be viewed as racist, ageist, sexist, or classist. Use positive humor rather than negative humor.
12. Retain your professionalism. Remember that you are a professional peacemaker, not a professional comedian. Don't monopolize the process with your jokes.

Laughter is beneficial throughout most processes, but it is rarely heard in litigation, at least not to bring the spouses together. Collaborative team members should be encouraged to use humor appropriately and to follow their clients' leads when determining if laughter can be helpful during tough negotiations.

Adam B. Cordover is the managing attorney of Family Diplomacy: A Collaborative Law Firm. Mr. Cordover practices exclusively in out-of-court dispute resolution with a focus on collaborative divorce and family law.

He attended law school at American University in Washington, D.C., and simultaneously attained a master's in international affairs. He never imagined he would end up in family law, but he graduated in 2008 when the economy tanked. After a lengthy period trying to find work, he landed at a family law firm. At first, he really could not imagine spending the rest of his life in the divorce field. But the more he worked with families, and especially when he discovered collaborative practice, he realized that his training in international relations (establishing common ground rules, building foundations of trust, interest-based negotiations, and delicate diplomacy) was very relevant to his practice in domestic relations.

Adam was fortunate in that the first landlord he had after hanging his shingle was a huge proponent of collaborative practice. Joryn Jenkins, from whom he rented office space, brought him into collaborative practice. She repeatedly suggested that he attend a collaborative training, but he was hesitant to pay an expensive registration fee or to take two days away from billing. Besides, he figured he was already a pretty friendly guy, and he always tried to be "nice" in his cases, except when he couldn't be. But Joryn was persuasive and dragged him, somewhat kicking and screaming, to his first collaborative training. He is so grateful that she did, as he has now built his entire practice around the collaborative process and other forms of private dispute resolution.

Mr. Cordover also trains attorneys, mental health professionals, and financial professionals on how to offer and excel in the collaborative process. He is a founding member of the Tampa Bay Collaborative Trainers, with whom he teaches family law professionals the basics of how to help spouses privately and respectfully resolve disputes via the collaborative process, and the Peacemaking Practice Trainers, with whom he teaches family law professionals how to make peacemaking their day job.

Additionally, Adam is a former president of Next Generation Divorce, a 501(c)(3) organization with collaborative members in Hillsborough, Pinellas, Pasco, Sarasota, and Manatee counties.

You can reach Mr. Cordover at Adam@CordoverLaw.com or at (813)443-0615. Visit his website at http://FamilyDiplomacy.com.

Even when a professional "wins" a litigated family case, the professionals and the client typically walk away feeling that they have lost. In reality, often, they have. If the vast majority of a family's savings has gone toward divorce attorneys' and experts' fees, even if the client received the few assets that she wanted, it is hardly a win for her and her family. And while it is arguably a "win" for the attorneys and experts who earned nice fat paychecks, if those professionals have any moral sense, they will feel guilty for leaving the family with almost nothing, no matter how hard they worked.

While legal professionals have certain ethical obligations to their clients, they are not committed to the fundamental guideline "First, do no harm" that is followed by the medical community. Many family litigants conclude their cases in much worse shape than they started, with their families in worse turmoil and having fewer assets. However, in collaborative practice, teams work together to leave the entire family in a positive financial position, with important relationships intact. – Ed. Note

FIRST, DO NO HARM
BY AUDREY JEFFERIS, ESQ.

When family lawyers litigate cases, even when a case is "won," have we failed our clients if we have not first analyzed the case pursuant to *primum non nocere*?

Primum non nocere is a basic medical precept; it means, "First, do no harm." Every medical student in the world learns this fundamental concept. Even if the treatment option will cure the targeted disease, will it cause another? Will it initiate terrible suffering for the patient? What are the potential side effects? Medical providers have an ethical duty to analyze whether a treatment will cause more harm than good for their patients. If so, they have an ethical duty to inform their patients and to discourage them from undergoing the treatment.

This fundamental ethical consideration in the field of medicine has no direct parallel in the traditional practice of law. While lawyers are required to analyze issues from an ethical standpoint, the purpose is usually only to determine the strength or weakness of the matter, not the potential impact or "harm" to the client or the children.

Instead, lawyers analyze the financial risks to clients and the likelihood of winning. For example, is this a frivolous or meritless action? Is it likely that the case will be won or lost? If the case is lost, will the client be required to pay attorney's fees or damages to the other party?

It is the lawyer's ethical duty to discuss the downfalls of litigation at the outset. He should advise the client of the inherent risks, the usual delays, the many expenses, the probable outcome, and the negative consequences of litigation. This should be done in much the same way as a medical provider helps a cancer patient to understand the limitations and implications of a given treatment.

If a patient is 75 years old and still intends to smoke two packs of cigarettes a day, is chemotherapy really a good option? Likewise, if a client wants residential custody or majority timesharing with a child but doesn't have the skills to include the other parent in the life of the child, is it really a good idea to litigate—even if the client wins?

Most clients do not understand the limitations of taking a family law case to trial. They believe that, if they have the opportunity to tell their side to the judge, the judge will have no other choice than to find that they are right. They are anxious and eager for the perceived vindication that will accompany the telling of their story.

The reality of the courtroom, however, is usually far less satisfying than anticipated. Time limitations, the rush to get through the testimony in the time allotted, and objections to the content of the testimony often leave parties feeling as if they haven't had the opportunity to "tell their side" or that they haven't been heard or understood. This happens even if the party "wins" a case or key issue in a family law matter.

A "win" in the context of a family law case may consist of an award of residential custody and majority timesharing with a child, an award of alimony, the award of an important asset, or an award of attorney's fees. It is difficult for people to understand that this "win" may be subject to modification in the future. It is not an award of rights without conditions on present and future conduct. Worse yet, in the case of children and some forms of alimony, it is a "win" that can be litigated again if there is a change in circumstances.

Furthermore, in complex or high conflict family law cases, it is not unusual for years to pass before the trial. Savings accounts and retirement funds are often liquidated to pay for the litigation. The couple and their children often suffer sustained emotional distress as a result of the delay and the financial burden. These factors diminish the "win."

The collaborative approach stands in stark contrast to litigation because the most important focus is the wellbeing of the client and the mitigation of harm. In a collaborative process, the divorce still happens, but the focus is not on winning and losing. The goal of the team and the clients is on reaching an amicable settlement that preserves the wellbeing and quality of life of the participants and their children.

The collaborative attorney and the other team members must take into consideration the potential harm to the spouses and their family from the outset. A team of skilled professionals analyzes and comes together to enable clients to find a workable solution. The professionals do not impose their will on the clients, but, instead, respect and consider their culture, lifestyle, and desires.

In a collaborative divorce, each client gets to tell his or her side of the story, not in order to "win," but to be understood and to be regarded. Resolving difficult issues is a process that requires the professionals to analyze and re-analyze the wellbeing of the clients. And it requires the clients to problem solve. If everyone on the collaborative team focuses on reaching a mutually acceptable solution, the process creates a pathway for healing.

I have no doubt that the successful collaborative matters upon which I was fortunate enough to be a team member have benefitted the clients and their children. I believe strongly that my clients who have participated in successful collaborative matters will not need my services in the future. They also have the resources of all of the team members who know their circumstances and the clients quite personally. My clients who have engaged in successful collaborative divorces tend to reach out to me periodically for legal advice and guidance, but they don't have unrealistic goals or demands.

The most rewarding aspect of the collaborative process is that, with the right team, everyone works together to reach solutions that minimize the risk of harm to the clients and their families. In this environment, everyone's wellbeing is taken into account, laying the groundwork for a healthier future.

Audrey Jefferis has been practicing law in Florida since 1995. She attended Bowling Green State University in Ohio and double majored in music and philosophy. She is board certified in marital and family law by the Florida Bar, has been a certified family law mediator since 2001, and is a trained and experienced collaborative professional.

Ms. Jefferis' practice is limited exclusively to family law, and she is dedicated to helping her clients make family transitions in the healthiest way possible. She became a family law practitioner because she was (and remains) fascinated by how humans treat each other, especially in our most intimate relationships. She has never viewed litigation as a good choice for her clients. She loves to help people solve problems and get through difficult times, so collaborative practice was a natural fit for her.

Ms. Jefferis loves western art music, jazz, and folk music from around the world. She volunteers at Big Cat Rescue as a keeper and hopes to one day volunteer at animal preserves around the world. In addition to her love of music and animals, she is an avid outdoorswoman who would rather be in a tent than in a fine hotel. She and her husband enjoy hang gliding, sailing beach catamarans, hiking the wilderness, and paddling on remote rivers and waterways.

Ms. Jefferis is pleased to provide collaborative family law services throughout the Tampa Bay area. You may view her website at www.floridafamilydivorce.com, and you may reach her at Audrey_Jefferis@AudreyJefferis.com.

When participating on a collaborative team, it is important to consider the core values of the clients and of the professionals. Understanding those of the clients will help the professional to better formulate settlements with which they will be happy and that will address any specific issues they may have revolving around their spirituality and religion.

Further, understanding the core values of the other professionals on your team will help you to more effectively work with them.

If you learn about a client's core values early on, offer to include team members who share similar values. Your client will appreciate that you are not only listening to what is really important to her, but are also trying to situate her as comfortably as possible in a room that includes like-minded professionals. – Ed. Note

CORE VALUES AND DIVORCE
BY SHANNON GREEN, CPA, CFE

Spirituality or religious views are often personal and private. Sometimes, however, differences in core beliefs can be the very cause of dissention between married couples.

I am divorced. I have strong religious beliefs, and my ex-spouse does not. I believe in raising our children with Christian teachings and theology, and, prior to our having children, my ex-spouse agreed that I could, despite his lack of religious beliefs. Once our daughter was born, he changed his mind and would not allow me to take her to church.

As someone who has attended church with my family twice a week since I was born and into adulthood and who feels the church's teachings are incredibly valuable, I wanted to impart them to our daughter. When my husband prohibited me from doing so, it created a huge divide between us, and my resentment increased.

Our different core values caused our separation and, ultimately, our divorce.

One of the ten most common reasons people get divorced is because, over time, they develop different priorities and interests.[1] "Having shared interests and exploring them together is essential for a successful marriage . . . unless you can find common passions and look for ways to experience them together, you'll inevitably grow farther and farther apart." Spirituality is a component of our core values. If two people don't have similar beliefs or mutual respect for their differences, the marriage may be doomed.

"Religious beliefs and cultural values can cause conflict, which affects the way you live your life and raise your children. If you aren't committed to adapting and practicing these values, this can be an ultimate deal breaker."[2]

When seeking to help our clients, we should consider their core values, spirituality, and/or religious beliefs. In many disciplines, this kind of discussion would be considered taboo. However, as collaborative professionals, it is important as people struggle to understand, accept, and ultimately work through the divorce process.

Dr. Kim Costello, a brilliant facilitator with whom I've been blessed to collaborate on several occasions, explains that the role core values play is two-fold. Firstly, they help people get through the process. As part of Dr. Costello's initial intake with her clients, she asks, "What are your personal core values? What would you like to pass on to your children?" She believes that understanding these is a key part of the intake process.

So, how can we define and understand our core values? The values we hold have been given to us as a means of living sincerely.

Dr. Martin Seligman, the founder of the positive psychology movement, has identified the character strengths, or core values, that have endured the test of time and are valid across all nations

---

[1] Payne, Lisa L., Olver, Kim, and Roth, Deborah. "The 10 Most Common Reasons People Get Divorced," The Huffington Post (September 16, 2015).

[2] Slupski, Brian. "The Top 10 Reasons Marriages End in Divorce," Marietta Patch (February 12, 2014).

and cultures.[3]

1. Creativity [originality, ingenuity]: thinking of novel and productive ways to conceptualize and do things; includes artistic achievement, but is not limited to it.
2. Curiosity [interest, novelty-seeking, openness to experience]: taking an interest in ongoing experience for its own sake; finding subjects and topics fascinating; exploring and discovering.
3. Judgment [critical thinking]: thinking things through and examining them from all sides; not jumping to conclusions; being able to change one's mind in light of evidence; weighing all evidence fairly.
4. Love of Learning: mastering new skills, topics, and bodies of knowledge, whether on one's own or formally; obviously related to the strength of curiosity but goes beyond it to describe the tendency to add systematically to what one knows.
5. Perspective [wisdom]: being able to provide wise counsel to others; having ways of looking at the world that make sense to oneself and to other people.
6. Bravery [valor]: not shrinking from threat, challenge, difficulty, or pain; speaking up for what is right even if there is opposition; acting on convictions even if unpopular; includes physical bravery, but is not limited to it.
7. Perseverance [persistence, industriousness]: finishing what one starts; persisting in a course of action in spite of obstacles; "getting it out the door;" taking pleasure in completing tasks.
8. Honesty [authenticity, integrity]: speaking the truth, but more broadly, presenting oneself in a genuine way and acting in a sincere way; being without pretense; taking responsibility for one's feelings and actions.
9. Zest [vitality, enthusiasm, vigor, energy]: approaching life with excitement and energy; not doing things halfway or halfheartedly; living life as an adventure; feeling alive and

---

[3] Scherrer, Joe. "Founded in Strength: 24 Core Values to Guide Your Leadership," (March 27, 2013).

activated

10. Love: valuing close relations with others, in particular, those in which sharing and caring are reciprocated; being close to people.

11. Kindness [generosity, nurturance, care, compassion, altruistic love, "niceness"]: doing favors and good deeds for others; helping them; taking care of them.

12. Social Intelligence [emotional intelligence, personal intelligence]: being aware of the motives and feelings of other people and oneself; knowing what to do to fit into different social situations; knowing what makes other people tick.

13. Teamwork [citizenship, social responsibility, loyalty]: working well as a member of a group or team; being loyal to the group; doing one's share.

14. Fairness: treating all people the same according to notions of fairness and justice; not letting personal feelings bias decisions about others; giving everyone a fair chance.

15. Leadership: encouraging a group of which one is a member to get things done, and at the same time, maintaining good relations within the group; organizing group activities and seeing that they happen.

16. Forgiveness: forgiving those who have done wrong; accepting the shortcomings of others; giving people a second chance; not being vengeful.

17. Humility: letting one's accomplishments speak for themselves; not regarding oneself as more special than one is.

18. Prudence: being careful about one's choices; not taking undue risks; not saying or doing things that might later be regretted.

19. Self-Regulation [self-control]: regulating what one feels and does; being disciplined; controlling one's appetites and emotions.

20. Appreciation of Beauty and Excellence [awe, wonder, elevation]: noticing and appreciating beauty, excellence, and/or skilled performance in various domains of life, from nature to art to mathematics to science to everyday

experience.

21. Gratitude: being aware of and thankful for the good things that happen; taking time to express thanks.
22. Hope [optimism, future-mindedness, future orientation]: expecting the best in the future and working to achieve it; believing that a good future is something that can be brought about.
23. Humor [playfulness]: liking to laugh and tease; bringing smiles to other people; seeing the light side; making (not necessarily telling) jokes.
24. Spirituality [faith, purpose]: having coherent beliefs about the higher purpose and meaning of the universe; knowing where one fits within the larger scheme; having beliefs about the meaning of life that shape conduct and provide comfort.

It is vital to know your values, be grounded in them, and use them regularly. Your signature strengths make you unique and give you something special to offer the world.

You can use this link to identify your client's core values. https://www.viame.org/survey/Account/Register.

Team members must, of course, be cautious about discussing religion or faith. Because of the separation of church and state, discussions about faith approach a sensitive line. In this touchy area, you must be aware of and sensitive to the boundaries regarding religion.

However, that doesn't mean you must avoid the topic. Some clients incorporate spirituality and faith in their parenting plan. This is common when spouses have different belief systems. For example, if one client is Jewish and the other is Christian, it is important to plan timesharing so that each spouse can celebrate the appropriate religious holidays with the children.

The second way core values work in the process is when a client is in dire distress. Dr. Costello may ask, "What or who do you have in your support circle? Do you go to church or Bible study?" If she knows they have spiritual beliefs, she sometimes brings in resources to help. In one case, the wife knew of Dr. Costello's faith and asked her if they could pray together before a collaborative meeting. Dr. Costello believes that meeting a client where he is comfortable and asking him key questions helps her to ascertain what gives him peace.

Even if spirituality is not part of a client's core values, perhaps they believe in the adage, "do unto others as you want done unto you." Because values differ from person to person, consider where the clients' values align and where they differ.

Dr. Costello draws on this information to help clients get back on track when they've been hurt or acted out in a way at odds with their beliefs. One of her clients would send her husband nasty text messages at night when she knew he was with his girlfriend. Dr. Costello reminded her of one of her core values, integrity, thus gently showing her that the behavior was out of sync with what she valued.

Incorporating core values into your intake form opens a conversation that prompts clients to think about their beliefs. Reviewing it allows you to get to know them more deeply, which can be helpful later when discussing options.

Core values direct clients to interests and away from positions, the heart of how the collaborative process works. The participation agreement which details client behavior should be reviewed during tough times in the process. Here are a few examples of various core values from the collaborative participation agreement:

1. We agree to effectively and honestly communicate with each other.
2. All written and verbal communications will be respectful and constructive.
3. Joint meetings will focus on those issues necessary to the constructive resolution of the matter.
4. We agree not to engage in unnecessary discussions of past events.
5. The clients acknowledge that inappropriate communications can be harmful to their child[ren].
6. Communication with the minor child[ren] regarding the matter will occur only as agreed by the clients.
7. Our goal is to reach an agreement that promotes the best interests of the child[ren].

Clearly, these guidelines align with various core values.

Spirituality and religious beliefs can be core values. As a professional, you must allow your client to disclose their values, and if spirituality or religious beliefs are important, you can use them as a guideline. It is wise to allow our own spirituality to make itself known naturally and not as something we actively introduce.

In determining core values, ask, "Where do you turn when you feel hopeless? Are you aligning with your core values?" The answers may be something that you can use to refocus your client when he is getting off track.

These considerations can play a significant role in the collaborative process. This knowledge enables us to achieve our goals and to eliminate the negative economic, social, and emotional consequences of litigation, and to reach an acceptable resolution.

Shannon Green is a certified public accountant in Florida and California and a certified fraud examiner with over 15 years of experience in forensic accounting. She earned a bachelor's degree in accounting at Illinois State University in Bloomington, IL, in 1994 and maintained a perfect 4.0 GPA in all accounting-related courses. That same year, Ms. Green received the distinguished "Airman of the Year" award with the United States Air National Guard.

Ms. Green served in the US military from 1990 to 1995 when she was honorably discharged. Upon graduation from USAF basic training, she was awarded the Honor Graduate designation, which is given to the top graduate in the class.

Ms. Green began her career with State Farm Insurance Companies at their corporate headquarters in Bloomington, IL, as a supervising financial systems accounting analyst. She then joined the internationally-recognized forensic accounting firm of Hagen, Streiff, Newton & Oshiro.

Ms. Green currently is a manager of forensic accounting at Harper Forensic CPAs. Over the last four years, she has completed approximately 80 hours of continuing education directly related to fraud and forensic accounting, investing, accounting for business, time value of money, and ethics. Ms. Green is a member of the American Institute of Certified Public Accounts and Association of Certified Fraud Examiners.

In addition to her eclectic and impressive work experience as a financial professional, she also has experience in family law matters, including alimony, child support, and equitable distribution. Ms. Green completed an intensive two-day introductory training course in September 2015, which meets the standards set by the International Academy of Collaborative Professionals (IACP) in interdisciplinary collaborative practice. She has worked on multiple collaborative matters and co-authored a web-based article "Collaborative Divorce in the Golden Years" posted March 30, 2016. She is a member of the IACP and attended the IACP conference in Las Vegas in October 2016.

Ms. Green may be reached at shannoncpa4@yahoo.com or at sgreen@tampaforensic.com.

Already vulnerable families are more susceptible to the devastation that can occur in divorce court. Without the support of a team of professionals, these at-risk families in turmoil can be completely destroyed by the stress of litigation. Weak spouses and children can be further victimized by their antagonizers. Mentally ill spouses can be pushed to their breaking points, resulting in heartbreaking tragedy.

While the family described here may not have belonged in collaboration, it is hard to argue that the chaos of litigation helped them at all. This family may not have been a collaborative success. However, with a team of professionals (including at least one mental health professional), they would have been more likely to get the help they needed before it was too late. – Ed. Note

THE COURT AS A WEAPON
BY JANE GREEN, LCSW, BCD

When Lenore called me early Monday and said that her ten-year-old daughter Annie had not shown up for school that morning, my heart sank. Later in the day, she called again. "The police are here; they found Annie's and Edward's bodies."

Her worst fear had come true. So had mine.

As I was the court-appointed parenting coordinator, Lenore had called me, very upset, the weekend of January 11, 2013, to tell me that Edward had taken Annie out of town without telling her. Their parenting plan required each parent to give the other 14-days' notice for all out-of-state travel. All weekend, we had been on the phone and texting back-and-forth.

Although some say that parenting coordination is not a crisis process and that weekend contact with the parents is not necessary, I do not find that to be accurate. Most family law professionals, and even many of the judiciary, care enough about their clients to make themselves available when they know there is the possibility of a tragedy. On the Saturday night after Edward took Annie out of state, I requested an emergency status conference with the judge.

Edward was representing himself *pro se* (meaning he no longer had representation by an attorney). I could not reach Lenore's attorney, but I managed to contact her paralegal. The paralegal was unconcerned. "Oh, that's just Edward upsetting Lenore again, like he always does."

When I reached Edward, he dismissed Lenore's worries. "If she had listened to me and noticed what I got Annie for Christmas, she would have heard I was taking her to see snow for the first time. I bought Annie winter clothes and have mentioned to Lenore many times we were going zip lining in Atlanta!"

Edward uncharacteristically agreed to speak with Lenore to reassure her and even allowed Annie to speak with her several times over that weekend, which he normally would not do during his parenting time. Annie assured Lenore she was in Atlanta, she was zip lining, and she was having fun. It is difficult to say if she was *really* having fun as the little girl had already learned to hide her feelings from her father.

By that Monday morning, both Annie and her father were dead. Sometimes when a parent kills his child and then himself, it is called "filicide." In this case, Edward had shot her multiple times in the face and then used the last bullet to kill himself.

They were not in Atlanta, but in Ohio, a short distance from Edward's father's home. Edward had left a letter to his father inside the car. Edward's family later told the police that they had not known that Edward and Annie were in Ohio.

Annie was murdered by her father on January 13, 2013. She had just turned ten that December.

I had only received the order to be the parenting coordinator in the highly litigious Smith case two months earlier, on November 16, 2012. Annie had begun to resist going to see her dad and refused to speak with him on the phone. Edward blamed Lenore and refused to accept that Annie did not want to speak with him. By the time that I met them, they had been in court constantly for three years. Despite Lenore agreeing to a shared 50/50 parenting time, Edward continually filed motions, objecting to Annie's extracurricular activities and other issues that appeared to be excuses to continue the contact.

He had petitioned the court for a psychological evaluation of Lenore, alleging that she had "issues." The date of the report was February 24, 2010. The evaluation appeared to confirm my intuition that it was Edward who was the danger to Annie, not Lenore, with the evaluator reporting a pattern of control by Edward. He physically and emotionally abused both Lenore and her son, Jason, from her first marriage. Also, he had threatened to kill a guinea pig and, subsequently, the animal had "died suddenly."

Lenore scored "average" or "above average" in all respects. The only problem the evaluator noted was that her score on the Life Stress Domain Test indicated "significant life stress."

The evaluator reported,

> All of the psychological instruments suggest that [Lenore] shows no evidence of psychopathology or symptoms of a mental disorder. There is no evidence of substance abuse. However, she expends a great deal of energy in monitoring and preventing the outward experience of anger. Her parenting skills and childrearing attitudes fall in the average-to-above-average range.

The psychological evaluation included Edward's allegations. He had petitioned for full custody, claiming falsely that Lenore was a drug addict who worked as an exotic dancer. Lenore was an LPN attending school to obtain her RN, which she accomplished. The report noted that Lenore functioned intellectually in the high average range. The psychologist found no support for Edward's allegations.

The evaluator recommended a "parenting coordinator who is familiar with characteristics of power and control imbalance to assist them in child-focused communication and parenting," as well as a "highly structured parenting plan . . . to increase the likelihood that the parties will be able to resolve disputes outside of litigation and remain focused on the minor child." The evaluator further recommended that Lenore "enter psychotherapy to address issues of insecurity and low self-confidence, as well as to reinforce appropriate boundary setting in relationships. She remains rather naïve about the impact of choosing romantic partners with whom there is an apparent imbalance of power and control."

Very soon after my appointment as parenting coordinator, I met separately with each parent. I also met them once together and had one appointment with Annie, totaling just four visits before the filicide.

During my meeting with Edward, he blamed Lenore and had no insight into the influence that his own actions had on his daughter. He stared at me coldly. "You, like all others, fail to see through Lenore's lies and deceit. You, too, are fooled by her." Afterward, he explained that he was no longer coming back, in spite of the court order. His reason was, "You believe all of Lenore's lies, and I can no longer afford you."

I requested a non-emergency status conference to inform the court that Edward clearly intended to refuse to follow the order for parenting coordination. Although I normally informed the judiciary if a client refused to follow a court order, I felt intuitively that this father was severely mentally impaired. But one cannot cite intuition as a reason for requesting a judge to intervene. I did not feel that I had sufficient justification to ask for an emergency hearing. After all, they had been in court on a regular basis for three years since their divorce had been finalized in 2009.

During my first meeting with Lenore, she was quiet, yet strong. She provided documents and information about the highly litigious case. "I believe he's run out of money because he still constantly files motions regarding my parenting, but he no longer has an attorney."

Sensing signs that she had been a victim of violence, I encouraged her to open up. "Tell me more about your marriage to Edward. Was he good to you?"

"He was difficult in every way. For instance, he made me organize all of the canned goods in alphabetical order." She described a union that was intensely punitive, both emotionally and psychologically, making clear the potential for physical violence. It appeared that she had been living in fear of Edward for a very long time.

She continued, "I quickly realized that Edward just wasn't right. I eventually learned that he had a history of harming and killing pets and of emotional and psychological abuse."

"Was he ever violent to you or Annie?"

She answered quietly, "Yes. One weekend, I just had to get away from him. When I came back, he'd changed the locks on all the doors. I banged on the door, and, when Annie opened it, Edward appeared suddenly and began punching me, knocking me to the ground and kicking me. He picked her up and threw her over his shoulder. She didn't speak for a week."

"Did you ever get an injunction against Edward?"

"I did, but I dropped the domestic violence charges on the advice of my former attorney."

"Then why does the parenting coordination order state that there is 'No Domestic Violence' in this matter?" I asked.

"During mediation, we agreed to take the domestic violence out of the divorce as an issue. I didn't want to, but we weren't going to make any progress if I didn't agree." She looked down, ashamed. "No matter what my attorney or I did to work with him, he could not, he would not, stop fighting."

"What is Annie's relationship with her father like?"

Shaking her head, Lenore explained, "She doesn't want to spend time with him and I don't blame her. He refuses to allow her to go to extracurricular activities. He sprays her with Lysol when she visits his house after being with me. She's scared of him. He complains and files motion after motion because Annie refuses to call him when she's with me. But Annie doesn't want to speak with him. She cries and refuses to take the phone when I try to force her. I protect her and I don't tell him that she's afraid of him."

When I met with little Annie, she was dejected. She recounted a similar story to the one that her mother had told me as she sobbed. "I'm not allowed to bring a single thing from Mommy's home to Dad's home. Dad doesn't let me close my bedroom door or the bathroom door at his house. He sleeps in a room across the hall from me, and he's always watching me. It's creepy."

"Do you want to have contact with your dad?" I asked the shy, pensive girl.

"No. He's quietly evil." She shuddered. Her choice of words

stunned me.

Unfortunately, although Annie gave me no reason that would allow me to call the Department of Children and Families, she just sobbed so brokenly that I knew something was terribly wrong. I met Annie that first and only time the Thursday evening before she was taken out of state and murdered by her father.

This tragedy might have been averted if the psychologist who had performed the evaluation on the mother had alerted the court that it was necessary to do a psychological evaluation on the father. If Edward had allowed this, perhaps something could have been done to save Annie's life.

Lenore was doing all she could to communicate with him even as he drove the conflict. The pattern indicated he was unable to stop his revenge-motivated anger.

Because there was a shared parenting plan and the marriage was over, there was no reason to continue filing in court, but he still used the court as a weapon against Lenore. The courts are often used this way by litigious folk. However, in this case, he suffered from a mental illness, and Lenore and Annie were his victims.

It is likely Edward would never have agreed to a collaborative divorce as he really did not want to cooperate or have a working relationship with Lenore. In researching "filicide," I came upon the statement that when a male kills his child and then himself, it is usually based on "revenge." This appeared to be true in this tragedy.

This case illustrates that, although the collaborative process is the best approach for folks during a time of conflict and sadness, it does not suit all. However, even in a divorce that is "high conflict," when it seems obvious that one parent is unable to control his behavior, it is moral and ethical for the family law professionals to assume the role of a "mandated reporter" and state what is happening that is cause for concern. It could mean that tragedy like this one is avoided.

Jane Green attended Fordham University after working for many years as a legal assistant for the senior partner in a large law firm. She then attended Rutgers School of Social Work. After graduation, she worked at a hospital during the day and for a counseling center in the evenings. Upon obtaining her license in New Jersey in 1995, she began her private practice.

Ms. Green moved to Florida in 1997 with her two small daughters after the death of her husband. She helps people solve problems that seem insurmountable and uses kindness, caring, and professional training to help families and children.

Ms. Green has taken the custody evaluation (n/k/a social investigation) training from three different experts. She specializes both in writing reports to the court to help the judiciary make decisions and also in working with parents to find peace during the process. Ms. Green has been certified by the Supreme Court as a family law mediator and as a parenting coordinator and is a former board member and former president of the Family Court Professional Collaborative.

After the tragic incident described in Ms. Green's chapter, she began to research the horrifying phenomenon of filicide and found that it was far more common than she had known. Ms. Green's mission is to prevent any more suffering, anguish, anger, and murder due to the conflict and havoc experienced by families going through divorce or post-divorce. She helps people in the middle of the anger, acrimony, and despair created by divorce and custody problems to find peace and resolution.

Ms. Green took the collaborative training from Next Generation Divorce in May 2014 and felt instinctively that the process would benefit children, families, and parents.

Clients are not always whom they portray themselves to be at first. This can be especially scary when you think of putting a client on the stand in court. What new information will you hear when the other attorney starts asking your sweet client questions? Will you (and the judge) learn something that turns your model parent client into a monster? Or that makes you realize that your seemingly needy client doesn't really deserve that alimony for which you were fighting so hard?

In collaboration, you don't have to worry about what the other side will uncover about your client. The clients pledge to be transparent, meaning that they will disclose any information relevant to their divorce in any way. This honesty allows the professionals to help the clients work towards their true goals and interests rather than those that they think the judge wants to hear. This leads to more customized agreements, which lead to happier clients. – Ed. Note

It's Not Always What It Appears to Be
By Robert Kokol, CFP, CDFA, AEP, MBA

John and Mary each gave off a distinct vibe as soon as they entered a room. He seemed a bit aggressive, maybe due to his bald head and pointy nose, or maybe due to his painstakingly organized manner. Everything was just so, from how he dressed to the care with which he put meetings on the calendar of his brand-new iPhone. He was clearly the fast-paced entrepreneur.

In contrast, Mary seemed a bit sheepish. She worked a union job and appeared to have limited earning capability. It was not hard to feel sorry for her. It was difficult to ignore the impression that John was bullying Mary into divorce.

I was the financial neutral for their divorce. During my first private meeting with John, he explained his relationship with her.

"We met at a local bar soon after we graduated from college. Initially, she was a lot of fun, and we both agreed we wouldn't have children. We wanted to work hard, but we also wanted to play hard. We'd scuba dive on weekends and had a blast. But, as time went on, she slipped more and more into her own world. I began working harder, often because I didn't want to come home."

Mary and John had been married for 17 years with no children, and he wanted out. In fact, he had moved out a year earlier.

In the first full team meeting, we went over the team's engagement letters and collaborative agreement. Because Mary was a government employee, we could understand her concern with the overall price. John, on the other hand, seemed to have the mindset of "let's get it done at any cost." I wondered if he had a girlfriend, but that kind of information is not typically something that comes up in the first meeting.

We had a strong team. We all knew one another well, though we had not worked collaboratively together yet. As a neutral, I was a bit concerned that one attorney was more experienced than the other. I felt like the two would get along, but they were very different personality types—one stronger, one weaker.

We held the meetings at my rather small office, which had little room to spread out and get comfortable. The room, just large enough for six people, seemed to magnify every sentence, especially when a comment was made to get attention. Sometimes people speak to converse and other times they just want to be listened to.

One wall of the room was a large plate glass window. When the sun bore down on it and tensions rose, the temperature in the room seemed to go up too.

John kept asking, "Are we staying on schedule?"

Mary kept emotionally responding, "Is that what's really important here?"

The first meeting was tense. As a neutral, it was my responsibility to gather the financials from John and to work with Mary on hers.

The more time I spent with her, the more I questioned my take on their personalities. When I tried to help her, she often grew emotional and asked questions like "How am I going to pay my bills?" and "How long will he be paying me alimony?" She talked about her former job as a realtor, a commission-based position she left because of concerns her income would drop if the market slowed. Not really liking sales made the union job the way to go because she could count on a consistent paycheck.

The day after our first meeting, John emailed me every statement I needed. After my meeting with Mary, I appreciated his timeliness and efficiency.

At the second full team meeting the following week, Mary arrived 20 minutes early. I wondered if it meant I had done a good job with her one-on-one or if it was simply more convenient because she was coming right from her lunch break.

While we waited, Mary told me about her weekend kayaking trip with her best friend, Julie. I soon learned that this was not the type of kayaking during which you sip cold beer or white wine as you paddle. Rather, she enjoyed something closer to whitewater kayaking. For a quiet type, that surprised me.

Her voice was strong when she said, "Wow, was that fun!"

"What other weekend activities do you and Julie enjoy?"

Her excitement was clear. "We love to paintball, especially against the guys."

I had been a paintball aficionado back in my day, and said, "I know that it's not a game for the timid and shy. In fact, you typically leave a paintball session pretty black and blue."

"Oh, no! It's a blast, and we're pretty good at it!"

Despite her early arrival and initial better spirits, the meeting did not go well. The attorneys were becoming frustrated with her constant complaining. "I'm not receiving enough. John wants the divorce, not me!"

In reality, he wanted out so badly that he was giving up too much, too quickly. When we went over the asset schedule, strange items showed up on his list. John was from Albania and had a number of art objects from his family's former country. He spoke Albanian, and some of the books were in his native tongue. Some were marital gifts from family, and they were near and dear to him. He was the organized one and wanted these items delivered in the same perfect condition they had been in when he had left the marital home, while Mary was off on a girl's weekend.

The team thought having each one prepare an asset schedule

would be straightforward, but John and Mary seemed to have a lot of stuff, despite not having kids. In particular, John had the very first sports car he had ever bought. He was quite attached to it and could not bear to give it up. He had an old work car for the weekdays, but on the weekends, he was all about the convertible. It was 20-plus-years-old and often broke, but he had become proficient at fixing it. In fact, he kept a toolbox in the trunk just to be safe.

Although he rarely spoke negatively about Mary, she reamed him out regularly, and he just bit his tongue. His restraint may have been part of his upbringing, for few men would hold back from the tongue-lashing he received from her at every meeting.

We hoped that the third full meeting would be the last group meeting. Once again, Mary came early. I asked her. "What did you do this weekend?"

Smiling proudly, she replied, "I went to the shooting range."

Shocked, I said, "What kind of guns do you like to shoot?"

"I love Glocks, and I have a few guns of my own. I love to go to the range for target practice."

I was getting a more accurate read on her. Maybe her tears were designed to get sympathy from the team, which John had been quietly complaining about from the very beginning. Maybe she wasn't shy after all.

We were getting close to a settlement, but they were still arguing over their numerous arcade-style video games. John was the mechanical type and a computer geek, so he was able to fix them when they broke down. Some were worth serious money, some were not. We finally got them to agree to use a draft pick process to divide up the games and artwork. A full resolution seemed close.

At the fourth meeting, we discussed the logistics of John moving his items out of the home. Mary didn't trust him to take only what was his and became very emotional.

Our facilitator Diane went above and beyond, as is her nature, and agreed to be present when he moved out. He didn't seem like the kind of guy to take something that wasn't his, but he also wasn't the kind of guy who wanted Mary there when he was moving out.

Diane arrived the day the movers were scheduled. From the outside, the house seemed quite nice, but when she walked inside, she was shocked. According to her, and unknown to us, Mary was a hoarder.

Later, Diane described the place to the team. "She had piles of junk everywhere. The only safe place to walk was a small shrine that she had of their wedding pictures, which had never been touched, even after John had moved out. The rest of the home was pretty trashed. He seemed so embarrassed. There was nothing to say, but oh, there was plenty to do. After waiting two hours, the moving men never showed up."

Bad news for Diane! She helped John move all of his possessions into his U-Haul truck. She was his only chance to get his things out of the house.

Diane explained, "We had to climb over piles of trash all through the house. Where there were once expensive kitchen items on the counter, now there were pizza boxes and moldy food. Dishes were stacked in the sink and over the top of the counter. The bed had not been made, and the sheets appeared not to have been washed in weeks, possibly months.

We never found out if John was afraid of Mary, but her excitement about the gun range and shooting had to weigh on him. She was competitive and did not want to lose. He was divorcing her, and Mary was clearly hurt and angry. This divorce took place several years before we worried as much about gun violence. Today, our team probably would have had more concerns.

Did Mary have the capacity to shoot her guns? Absolutely. And she enjoyed the hobby.

Did John ask Diane to help move his things out of the house because he knew he would not get a second chance? Clearly.

Was Mary suffering from some form of mental illness? According to Diane, who was also a mental health professional, yes.

Did John know this? Probably. Once you got to know these folks, it was impossible to call it anything else.

Were there a whole lot of lessons learned in this matter? Absolutely.

First and foremost, never ever make an initial assessment of either client in a matter. You never know if you are seeing the genuine person or a façade. Give it time.

Also, anytime the second amendment is part of a passing conversation, put your antennas up. This is not about being judgmental but about keeping everyone safe.

Lastly, each spouse benefits from his settlement in his own way. John never wanted the house because he wanted to retire early. He just wanted his 401K and stock options. He also knew the house was a pigsty that needed a lot of TLC. Getting away from her was more important to him. The family photos and wedding gifts were the only things he really wanted and were not big numbers on the asset schedule. They had little, if any, intrinsic value.

It's not about the material value of the things, rather, it's the emotional value. It was about him getting what he really wanted from the marriage.

As one of my first collaborative matters, I learned that it is the clients' settlement. Let them negotiate in a manner that works for them and gives each of them what they really want.

Ultimately, Mary, the true competitor, demanded John pay the lion's share of the legal bill. That was her pound of flesh for him wanting the divorce. It hurt him. She knew it. He paid it.

Robert Kokol, CFP®, CDFA™, AEP®, MBA is a financial expert in Tampa, Florida, who has focused his practice in the divorce arena for over ten years. He has also maintained an investment and financial planning practice since 2004 and is one of the few financial planners to establish his own registered investment advisory to work with clients in the divorce arena, Divorce Financial Planning LLC.

Mr. Kokol is a Florida certified family law mediator. He also works with wives in divorce matters in an advocate capacity to "level the playing field." As their advocate, his job is to work with wives and their legal counsel in the negotiation process, usually in a mediation setting, to help them fully understand the financial decisions they are making. In addition, Mr. Kokol works with clients and their estate planning attorneys to rewrite their estate plan post-divorce purely from a financial perspective.

Mr. Kokol has served in numerous collaborative divorce matters as a financial neutral and, at times, as both the facilitator and financial neutral. He was elected the first non-lawyer co-chair of the Tampa Bay Academy of Collaborative Professionals, as well as president of the Tampa Bay Estate Planning Council.

Mr. Kokol's career began at SunTrust Bank as a financial analyst, and ultimately, as a senior commercial lender. In 1998, he moved to the trust department of SunTrust Bank where he worked successfully until 2003. After moving to Northern Trust in 2003 in a similar role, he went to Raymond James Trust, founding and heading their family office. Mr. Kokol has accumulated substantial expertise in the high net worth arena throughout his career.

You may reach Mr. Kokol at RKokol@GlobalFinancialPC.com.

Anyone contemplating divorce will likely have many questions. Professionals should be prepared to put their clients at ease by providing information in a way that is informative, yet not overwhelming. Attorneys have an ethical responsibility to explain the divorce process options to every consult so that he may choose the option that is most appropriate and cost-effective for his personal situation.

Many consults will also want to know what they can expect from the process, as well as what a court would likely consider them entitled to. Professionals should stress to clients that, while by looking at case law and statutes we can have a rough idea of what a court might award to a client, there are too many other variables at play to truly know how a case will be decided, from the personality and values of the judge to the way that the evidence is presented to the likeability of the client on the stand. Anything can happen when you go to court.

To truly have a say in one's future and in the life-changing decisions that are made in a divorce, clients should be encouraged to be the decision-makers in their own divorces by participating in alternative dispute resolution processes like collaboration rather than in litigation. – Ed. Note

DIVORCE: A TIME OF QUESTIONS AND UNCERTAINTY
BY KENNIE TAYLOR, CIMA®

Divorce signals not only the death of a relationship, a family, and a way of life, but it also involves splitting assets and liabilities and the emotional stress of determining how to divide time with children in a way that promotes their best interests. Even when clients understand that divorce is necessary, they often question how they should share their children, property, and debts. Surrounding them with a collaborative team of experts reduces their anxiety because the team's goal is to help the family reach a settlement that meets each client's most important interests. The team answers their questions to ensure that they understand what is happening and to help diminish their fears and uncertainties. The following are some of the most common questions clients ask during the divorce process.

"WHERE DO I START?"

Let's start at the very beginning. Most people initially want to know what to expect and where to begin. "How do I tell my spouse?" "How does the process start?" "What can I expect?"

The answers often lie in helping the client decide where she wants to end up. Does she hope to maintain a workable relationship with her ex? Is it important to her that her children not suffer through undue stress? Is she okay with not having her day in court or with her husband not coming out as a loser? If the answers are "yes," then a collaborative divorce is likely her best option. But be sure to explain each divorce process option so that she is able to make an informed choice.

In many marriages, there is a primary breadwinner and a primary caregiver. The non-breadwinning spouse often faces many financial challenges as one home is split into two. "Who will get what assets?" "How will income be divided?" "How will I pay my bills during the divorce?" "Who will pay for my children's school, clothes, and summer vacations?" Advise her that being prepared can help things go more smoothly, reduce her stress, and protect her financial interests.

Most non-breadwinner spouses find divorce frightening and intimidating because they worry that they will be taken advantage of if they don't fully understand the family's finances. These fears can keep that person in an unhealthy, unnerving, and unfulfilling relationship.

For some, the other spouse uses the threat of removing one's financial security as a weapon or means of control to manipulate and inflict abuse. Concern that credit cards will be cancelled or bank accounts closed can paralyze the strongest of us. Suggest to such a consult that she consider freezing her credit profile at the major

96

bureaus so no new accounts can be opened in her name. To do so, she simply contacts them. There is generally little to no cost associated with this action.

Remind the non-breadwinning spouse that if she chooses a collaborative divorce, she will have a neutral financial professional to guide her, help her gather her discovery, and make schedules of financial proposals for settlement.

The breadwinning spouse who didn't have many caregiving responsibilities faces different concerns. He loves his children, but he doesn't know if he is equipped to care for them without his wife. He is also concerned that a judge will not allow him ample time with his children and that his ex will be able to control when he sees them. Remind this client that a mental health professional, and sometimes a child specialist, is included on the collaborative team. These people are trained in the developmental needs of children and understand that, in most instances, children do better when they have two loving parents involved in their lives.

This spouse will also be concerned that his wife will "take everything" from him. Remind him of the role of the financial professional. The FP supports not just the client with little financial knowledge but also the primary wage earner and can suggest settlements that maximize the couple's income and assets.

"WHAT IS FAIR?"

The question I dislike the most is, "What is fair?" Although I understand why clients ask this question, when it comes to divorce, there is really no such thing as "fair." I generally respond, "'Fair' will be out of town when you look for it, and 'equal' never shows up." These are harsh realities in a litigated divorce.

"Fair" is usually defined as what the couple agrees to do or what the judge tells them to do. Hopefully, they can agree on a tolerable framework. Working together with the help of a collaborative team, mediators, attorneys, and/or counselors will generally prepare the couple with insights that will help them heal after the divorce.

However, if the judge is forced to make the decisions and define "fair," they should be prepared for a fight. A judge and attorneys will never know the facts and details as well as the couple does. Sadly, this brawl takes place in public, and the results are commonly damaging, especially if children are involved.

In a collaborative divorce, "fair" is a resolution that satisfies the couple's highest priorities in a way upon which both can agree.

"WHAT DO I DO NEXT?"

An individual involved in a divorce should assess and prioritize what is most important to her. Make no mistake, adjustments will have to be made to support two households on the same amount of total income. Even if a couple makes $1 million a year in income, it does not magically become $2 million after a divorce.

In the vast majority of matters, proper planning is the next step. Ideally, during times that are calm, each spouse can come up with possible plans that are viable and emotionally palatable. Clear thought is more likely to lead to a financially sound plan. The good news is that there is seldom one right answer. In the end, it's what works for the couple and what is realistic with the resources available to the family.

The best way to prepare a client is to make sure that she understands the necessary changes in the standard of living. The key is to minimize that change in a way that gives her confidence and peace of mind. Ask questions like: "Do you work now?" "Do you have skills that could be put to work for you in the workforce?" "If not, could you enhance or retrain to be competitive in the job market?" Advise her that potential post-marital support can be impacted if it appears that she is deliberately underemployed in an attempt to get more support.

In a litigated process, each spouse's attorney gathers financial data from his client and they exchange that information. Many attorneys and clients play "hide the discovery" games and employ battling experts, which drives up fees.

In contrast, in a collaborative process, one financial professional, who typically bills at a lower hourly rate than the attorneys do, gathers all the data from each spouse and then provides each attorney with the information. Collaborative divorces are often less expensive than litigated divorces, in part because the clients pay one person at a lower hourly rate, rather than two.

Advise your client, "You can either put your kids through college or your attorney's kids through college."

"WHAT WILL I HAVE TO SPEND?" AND "WILL MY LIFESTYLE CHANGE?"

In simple terms, the level of support after the divorce is generally calculated by looking at each person's expenses and income. Encourage your client to work on a budget, a good and necessary tool for evaluating current and future spending. The professionals will worry about the effects of things like taxes and inflation.

A successful budget contains all the financial data, including income, expenses, and incidentals. The bill payer in the marriage will likely have this information readily available, but the other spouse may need more help, especially if she doesn't have access to online accounts or paper statements. The transactions from an individual's financial history will give her a sense of current cash flow and a frame of reference for the cost of maintaining the lifestyle she enjoyed while married.

A budget should include every expenditure, large and small, in order to create a map of where her money needs to go. Provide her with a detailed worksheet to use so that nothing is overlooked. Next, have her put these expenses into categories of needs and wants or "non-discretionary" and "discretionary" items. Examples of non-discretionary items are health insurance premiums, groceries, and fuel. Discretionary items are vacations, a second vehicle, and jewelry. Gray areas could be purchasing a new BMW that is replacing a four-year-old Honda or the cost of private high school versus attending a public one. Whether the item falls into wants or needs, remind your client that she can only spend each dollar once.

Tracking actual spending is the next step. People often think they spend quite differently than they do, so it is helpful to see where the deviations are. It serves as a cross-check, confirming certain categories and bringing to light others that need adjusting.

Treat this as a working document, not something set in stone. There is no substitute for taking enough time to carefully estimate post-marriage spending.

Housing can be a difficult area to estimate, especially when the client will be moving out of the marital home. Despite that many people would prefer to stay in the home, unless the couple is living substantially below their means, the reality of having two homes is seldom possible without significantly altering spending elsewhere. Most clients know their monthly mortgage payment and property taxes, but far fewer can accurately estimate the cost of annual insurance, maintenance, and upkeep.

Clients should prepare their budgets with a pencil and paper unless their techy expertise makes using a spreadsheet or computer program easier for them. Consider employing a planning-based financial professional because CPAs or forensic accountants use a very different set of skills. Financial professionals aim to see a probability of 85-90% that a client will reach her vision of financial success.

"WHAT HAPPENS DOWN THE STRETCH?"

The client should focus on reaching an agreement and staying out of the courtroom. She should pull her credit reports and look carefully for any open items that are in her name, with or without her spouse, so that there aren't any surprises after the decree is finalized. Overdraft protection lines of credit are often overlooked because they frequently are dormant until needed. Also, zero balances don't mean the accounts are closed. Be careful when advising a client to close accounts, as this may lower her credit score.

Encourage clients to be creative and think outside the box when contemplating settlements. I often hear things like, "I am not paying him any *^#@+* alimony!" Or, "I am not giving her the *^#@+* house!" If the support guidelines indicate that a spouse should get support, but the other spouse refuses to pay it, he may be more willing to give the entitled spouse more assets or take on more liabilities in exchange for an alimony waiver. Perhaps the client will consider selling the house and putting the proceeds on the table for settlement.

Housing post-judgment can be a sticky issue, especially if

mortgages are involved. Some lenders are more flexible than others when they consider spousal support for loan qualification. Connecting your client with a mortgage broker who is familiar with divorce issues can be useful and help your client avoid unintended complications. This is another benefit of keeping the decision out of the judge's hands, so do what you can to get an agreement, and encourage your client to be creative, cooperative, and collaborative.

"WHAT TAKES PLACE AT THE FINAL JUDGMENT?"

A client tells her attorney 100% of the facts that she believes best represent her case. The attorney understands and remembers a percentage of what the client said. Her attorney tells the other attorney the facts as he remembers it, and the other attorney remembers a percentage. The judge gets those facts and remembers a percentage. Finally, that state employee (the judge) uses only the percentage she deems relevant to decide your case. So, that is a percentage, of a percentage, of a percentage, of a percentage of the facts a client told her attorney that will be used to set the course for the rest of her life. This is why I chose a customized collaborative process for my own divorce, and why I advise clients to do so as well.

"WHAT DO I DO POST FINAL JUDGMENT?"

This phase is not a sprint, but a marathon. Provide your client with a checklist for everything. After several months, she should pull her credit report again to make sure everything is as it should be. She should consider a credit monitoring service for a year. She must re-title her accounts pursuant to the terms of the final judgment. Advise her that distribution from retirement accounts have specific rules so that taxes are not levied, especially plans like 401(k)s. She should review all beneficiary designations on life insurance and annuity contracts and update her personal estate documents with her new status in mind. These items should be taken as "food for thought" as opposed to an exhaustive list. The process can be tedious, but encourage your client to be patient and work her way down her checklists.

I strongly recommend that anyone who is ending his or her marriage sit down with a professional or a team of professionals while navigating the hurricane called "divorce." This generally results in a better divorce experience and better planning for a higher quality post-divorce life.

Kennie Taylor, CIMA® watched his younger sister suffer through a very painful, traditionally litigated divorce and felt the emotional toll it took on her and on his entire family. After watching his sister's experience, he vowed to apply his expertise as a financial advisor to help women facing divorce find their ways to better outcomes.

The personal experiences of his life are natural bridges to the strong connections he has with his clients. Growing up as the middle child between two sisters has helped him relate to women. He is proud of his mom and sisters—all strong women, who manage the money in their households.

Experiencing how a difficult traditionally litigated divorce negatively affected his younger sister and his entire family, Mr. Taylor knew that there must be a better way, especially when children are involved. He truly sees the value in cooperative and collaborative processes that remove the courtroom entirely.

Mr. Taylor understands the devastating effects divorce can have on the finances of women. It is why he is a proponent of cooperative and collaborative divorces, where couples seek to arrive at mutually agreed-upon settlements through negotiation. An alternative to the traditional court-based divorce, it can save time, money, and the destruction of litigation.

He believed so much in the collaborative process, after going through the required introductory and multiple optional advanced trainings, that he used it for his own divorce. His goal was to preserve his relationship with his son and to be on the best terms as possible with his son's mother. By avoiding the attack and combat tactics that accompany going to court and approaching their separation in a cooperative way, both he and his son's mother have been able to maintain a healthy relationship with their son and each other.

Mr. Taylor is currently enrolled in the Certified Divorce Financial Analyst® curriculum and has more than 24 years of experience in the financial services industry. As a Certified Investment Management Analyst®, he applies state-of-the-art investment theory to provide objective investment advice and guidance to individuals and institutions. He has met extensive experience and ethical requirements, in addition to successfully completing advanced investment management consulting coursework through the Wharton School, University of Pennsylvania. He is a graduate of the University of Michigan, and he attended Adrian College.

If you'd like to contact Mr. Taylor, please e-mail him at Kennie.Taylor@RaymondJames.com.

For most families, expense is a concern when deciding which divorce option to choose. Because of all of the professionals involved in a collaborative divorce, it can seem like an option only available to the wealthy. Full team meetings can cost approximately $1,000 to $1,500 per hour depending on the hourly rates of the professionals and the number of professionals involved. It's understandable that most families will feel that it is not an option for them.

When compared with the expense of litigation, however, collaborative is often a more affordable choice. Collaborative divorces typically take much less time than litigated matters. The longer that a matter is unresolved, the more attorneys' fees will be spent. Also, in litigated divorces, high-billing attorneys normally do all the work, even in areas in which they do not specialize, like preparing financial schedules and parenting plans. In collaborative divorce, financial and mental health professionals, who generally bill at lower hourly rates, do this work. Plus, it is work in which they have been specifically educated, so they perform it more effectively, leading to fewer post-judgment issues. Moreover, in collaboration, clients aren't paying for battling experts or for discovery games.

Collaboration just makes good sense! – Ed. Note

DOLLARS AND SENSE OF DIVORCE
BY DENA THOMPSON-ESTES, ESQ.

Knock, knock. Who's there? Time. Time who? Time will tell.

When I meet you in an initial consultation, you will inevitably ask, "How long will my divorce take?" and "How much will it cost me?"

Time is relative to cost. Traditional litigated divorces can cost each person $5,000 to over a $100,000 and can take anywhere from a few months to a few years, especially if the parties battle over

CHANGING THE WAY THE WORLD GETS DIVORCED

custody, support, or property. Typically, a case moves forward as quickly as the slowest person, so an attorney cannot predict how long yours will take.

The amount of time varies based on the judge's schedule; the complexity of the issues; whether there are children, significant assets, and/or business interests involved; and your desire either to speed things up or to delay the process. If you focus on taking unreasonable positions, assigning blame, or not considering the best interests of your children, then the time and cost will significantly increase. A lengthy battle means higher fees while both spouses diminish their assets, leaving less to divide in the end.

Legal fees depend on several factors, such as the attorney's hourly rate, the area in which you live, whether your spouse and/or her attorney are amiable or aggressive, the issues involved, whether or not the case goes to trial, etc. A two- or three-day trial can cost each party as much as $25,000 in legal fees for the trial alone.

Marital and family law attorneys generally charge from $100 per hour to as much as $700 per hour for partners of a firm or board-certified lawyers. Most individuals pay between $150 and $350 per hour, with $250 being the average rate.

The legal fees accrued during the process do not include trial costs. Obviously, the fewer issues resolved ahead of time means a higher cost for resolving them at trial. Typically, attorneys charge an additional retainer fee to prepare for and attend the trial.

Other costs include hiring an accountant, a real estate appraiser, a parenting coordinator, or another necessary expert. Unless you have no income or low enough income to qualify for legal aid assistance, you will incur legal expenses. In some cases, you or your spouse will be required to pay all or some of the legal fees for the other. Litigated or contested divorces often force people to spend a significant portion of their hard-earned savings when these funds could be better used for retirement or their children's educational expenses.

Fighting, rather than compromising, always costs more, both emotionally and financially. People tend to fight out of principle, but the court will not compensate you based on principle. The court will follow the black letter of the law and only award you what you are legally entitled to; do not be penny wise and dollar foolish.

So, if you ask me the cost for a divorce, I will ask you, "To what costs are you referring? The cost of maintaining a good relationship with your soon to be ex-spouse? The cost of maintaining your lifestyle? The cost of your child's emotional wellbeing?" You must evaluate your values and interests when you go through a divorce. Nowadays, it costs just as much, if not more, to get divorced as it does to get married.

How can you avoid an astronomical price tag? Go collaborative! The average collaborative divorce lasts approximately six months, depending upon the availability of the spouses and their collaborative team. Highly emotional couples extend the time, but the neutral facilitator helps resolve difficult issues as quickly and as painlessly as possible.

The cost of a collaborative divorce is typically one-third of the cost of a traditional divorce if there are significant assets and complex issues involved, and you have a typical collaborative team (two attorneys, one neutral financial professional, and one neutral family professional, facilitator, or communications specialist).

On average, the cost may range from $5,000 to $15,000 per spouse. Generally, a collaborative divorce is less expensive financially and emotionally, but the cost savings depend on the clients' willingness to communicate and to compromise.

In one of my collaborative matters, the clients had no children but had significant assets. They decided the best way to handle their matter was by taking it into their own hands. After they educated themselves about the collaborative process, they consulted a marriage counselor to sort out their issues and non-issues and to narrow the focus on their true interests. Many therapists provide pre-divorce counseling. They provide an open and safe place for couples to discuss their finances, their interests, and, more importantly, how they envision their future after the divorce. This is an example of how to make a collaborative divorce work.

In addition to legal fees, there is the emotional cost. While custody or personal property issues may seem straightforward to you, there are often personal connections to these decisions. For example, you may want to keep the marital home because that is where your children grew up. Or you may not want to sell the family business that you created with your spouse.

One of the biggest and most important prices to be paid is the emotional impact on your children. The negatives and positives are up to you and your spouse. Having long, drawn out fights at home, making degrading remarks about each other in front of your children, and discussing the intimate details of your divorce with them are a few examples of behaviors during a divorce that can have detrimental effects on your children and that can leave lasting scars.

Children whose parents are going through a contentious divorce exhibit coping behaviors such as denial, anger, hostility, abandonment, depression, blame, and guilt. On the other hand, if you and your spouse are committed to being cooperative, respectful, and having an open dialogue, as is the case in collaborative divorces, then each family member will emerge relatively unscathed. This will allow you and your spouse to maintain a good relationship, not only for your own emotional wellness but also for the sake of your children. Remember, you are parents forever. You will be seeing your former spouse for years to come at graduations, weddings, and other life-changing occasions.

Another emotional cost in a litigated divorce is the "blame game." This is where you stop taking responsibility for your own actions and, instead, point fingers and lay fault solely on your spouse. It makes you focus your energy on the past when you should be thinking about the future.

Phrases like "You did it!" "You gave me no choice!" and "It's all your fault!" will only hurt your case. Your spouse's defenses will go up, as would yours, and she or he will naturally shut down and stop listening to anything you say. Not to mention you can kiss a fair agreement goodbye because your spouse will likely be spiteful during settlement negotiations.

Also, airing your dirty laundry to a room full of professionals or spewing it out on paper for the world to see is embarrassing for your spouse, and you should feel the same. It is fine to tell your attorney all of your grievances, but you should not do it in your spouse's face. There is truth to the old adage, "You can attract more flies with honey than with vinegar."

The longer your case drags on, the higher the cost, and the more

CHAMPIONS OF COLLABORATIVE DIVORCE

likely that bitterness will destroy your already tenuous relationship with your spouse.

In one of my cases, the wife blamed the husband for the downfall of their relationship because he had a vice of which she was fully aware throughout the marriage. It was not until they were in the collaborative setting that she voiced her outrage, which led to insinuations and what the husband felt were unreasonable demands.

The positive side to this situation was that the wife felt safe to speak up in the transparent and confidential atmosphere. Had the couple been in litigation, she likely would have filed motions with spiteful language and unsavory allegations. These would have become public record for anyone to read, including their children, and would have led to a scathing response filed by the husband. This is another example of how folks in a collaborative divorce function better than those involved in a traditional divorce, despite the wounds they have experienced.

Another emotional cost of litigation: it fosters position-based thinking rather than interest-based thinking. Position-based thinking allows each to focus solely on personal wants and needs, to take a stance, and to fail to find common ground. Interest-based thinking permits the couple to determine each other's underlying needs, goals, or concerns and to work together to satisfy them. Basically, it is *what* you want versus *why* you want it.

Your life is not black and white, and neither is your case. In the same way that life is full of various shapes and colors, you will have numerous options or solutions that you and your spouse can create and agree upon. Litigation gives people a false sense of security because they believe that the court will magically fix all of their problems and rule in their favor.

Litigation is often the result of bitterness or anger, which can lead to exhaustion. These hostile feelings can result in your case going to trial, an inequitable settlement agreement, or an impasse during settlement negotiations, which, in the end, will only increase mutual resentment. With these negative emotions driving you, you may be more likely to give in or to be bullied into agreeing to certain terms that you otherwise would reject.

"How can I reduce the emotional costs of divorce?" you ask. Get a collaborative divorce! This process allows you and your spouse to control the outcome rather than putting the fate of your lives in the hands of the judge, someone who is a stranger, who may not share your values, who does not have a vested interest in the results, and who does not have to live with the results of the ruling. There is no guarantee that you will win your position if you go to court. You are gambling with your life choices by allowing a judge to make your decisions.

Why gamble? The house always wins, not you! If spouses maintain the decision-making authority in a divorce, they will be happier once the divorce is finalized.

In one of my matters, the clients had children, but little income or assets. They flat out told us attorneys that they wanted to use those funds for their children's living expenses and future educational expenses, not legal fees. Because of their shared interest in their children, they selflessly put the needs and interests of their children before their own. By setting aside their positions and desires, they were able to focus on the bigger picture. They realized their goals to maintain an amicable relationship with each other for the sake of their children, to fairly divide all of their assets and debts, and to safeguard their children's financial future.

Collaborative divorce is not for everyone. The two people must want to maintain a friendly relationship after their divorce, especially if children are involved. If your spouse is naturally litigious, then he may not agree to participate in the collaborative process, may not be cooperative in the collaborative matter (which can cause the process to be terminated), or may not be satisfied no matter the end result. However, if the couple puts their emotions aside, actively listens to each other's goals and interests, shows respect for each other when they voice their opinions, and comes to the table with an open mind and willingness to compromise, then the couple has an opportunity for a win-win scenario. They will have a unique chance to save money, reduce tension, repair relationships, and protect their mental health.

With each passing day, you will realize that you must adjust to a new life as a divorced individual, no longer a part of a couple, but knowing that your life will, and *must,* go on.

So, the $64,000 question is . . . how do you want to get divorced?

Since 2004, Dena Thompson-Estes has worked exclusively in the area of marital and family law. She is experienced, diligent, and personable in her representation. As a product of divorced parents, she appreciates the difficulties of divorce and is sensitive to parents coping with their children's anxiety during this transitional time.

Her experience in family law cases includes complex and high net worth matters. She handles matters involving dissolution of marriage, equitable distribution, alimony, child support, timesharing, modification, enforcement, contempt, paternity, prenuptial and postnuptial agreements, and marital settlement agreements.

She is active in the following organizations: The Florida Bar, Hillsborough County Bar Association, The Stann W. Givens Family Law American Inn of Court of Tampa, International Academy of Collaborative Professionals, Next Generation Divorce, and the Carrollwood Area Business Association.

Ms. Thompson-Estes is also a Florida Supreme Court certified family law mediator and is trained in parenting coordination and interdisciplinary collaborative divorce. Her training has honed her negotiation skills to allow her to successfully resolve all types of issues that arise in contentious cases.

She and her husband have a passion for traveling, reading, and charity walk/run events. Their daughter, Hayden, who is nine months old as of this writing, is the light of their lives. Contact Ms. Thompson-Estes at DEstes@TheWomensLawGroup.com.

In any divorce, there are third parties who influence how the clients feel and how the matter will be resolved. Third parties can be romantic interests, parents, children, friends, neighbors, clergy, therapists, or employers—anyone who influences the client's decisions. Some of these third parties hinder the process by increasing hostility, delaying matters, and encouraging unreasonable resolutions, but many are beneficial because they ease stressed spouses and encourage emotional spouses to focus on the positives and to stay reasonable.

A spouse in a long-term marriage has been sharing important decisions with his spouse for many years and is often unable to make a decision on his own. A trusted third party can be crucial in helping the spouse to feel comfortable enough to agree to a resolution. Encourage your clients to lean on trusted third parties when they are helpful in resolving matters in a positive way. – Ed. Note

INVOLVING THE ADULT CHILD IN THE GRAY DIVORCE
BY DIANE RODRIGUEZ, LCSW

With the divorce rate for those 50 years old or over on the rise, it is not surprising that the couple from my first collaborative divorce matter fell into this demographic. This was a *pro bono* collaborative divorce involving an elderly couple with adult children. Because they had extremely limited resources and no computer, we did all of our work with them over the phone and in person.

Prior to accepting the matter, I reflected on whether I could remain neutral with clients who reminded me of my grandparents. Knowing their limited finances, how could I help? After much thought, I accepted the role as their neutral facilitator. The team consisted of two attorneys (counsel and co-counsel) for each client,

113

a financial neutral professional, and a neutral facilitator. Because it was the first collaborative divorce for all the professionals involved, we secured an experienced and dedicated mentor, Joryn Jenkins.

Ervin was a sweet, hard-working 79-year-old patriarchal man originally from Slovakia who loved to tell stories. He was a little hard of hearing and had a history of getting confused under stress. He was close to his grandchildren and spoke about them often.

Nusi was a pleasant, independent 70-year-old woman, also from Slovakia. Her strong accent made it clear that English was not her first language. She was hard of hearing, but she was also good at letting the team members know when she could not hear them.

When I met with Nusi prior to our first full team meeting, I immediately liked her. She was strong and confident, much like myself. "Nusi, tell me what initially attracted you and Ervin to one another."

"We both spoke Slovak. Being from the same area of the world, we shared the same traditions, histories, and culture."

"How long have you been married?"

"We knew each other about six months before we married, 46 years ago."

"Tell me about your marriage."

She paused before continuing. "We moved to Florida about six years into our marriage and never left. We lived by our Slovakian culture. We worked hard. We are proud people, and we don't believe in asking for help. Ervin was a certified air conditioning technician and had his own business. He was always a bit of a "workaholic." I never worked outside the home, but I did his bookkeeping. We had three children who are adults now."

"Tell me about them."

"Our son Frank lives in New York and isn't married. Our youngest daughter Eva is married and has two young children. She lives in Chicago. Our oldest daughter Jessica is married, but she doesn't have any children, at least not yet. She lives about an hour away, so we see her fairly often. She's always there when we need her. I don't know what we would do without her."

"What made you want to get a divorce?"

"We've talked about it for years, but it just never seemed right. Our culture really frowns on divorce, but I just couldn't take Ervin any more. He's been verbally abusive to me for years."

"What kinds of things does he say to you?"

"He calls me 'stupid woman' several times a day, almost like he considers it a term of endearment. He has no respect for the sacrifices I've made to stay at home and raise our family and take care of him. He thinks that, because he is the man, what he says goes."

"Has he ever been physically violent with you?"

"Never until about a year ago. He gets frustrated more easily now that he's older, and about a year ago, he slapped me."

"What did you do?"

"I called the police, and I kicked him out!"

"Did you get a restraining order?"

"No."

"So where does he live now?"

"He bought a house close to me, and I'm still living in our home. We've paid it off, and I'm comfortable there."

"Do you worry for your safety because he lives so nearby?"

"No. He actually still has a key to the house and comes over to visit daily. We usually share an early dinner together every day."

"Do you have any close friends?"

"No. Just my family."

"What's your biggest concern in your divorce?"

"I'm worried about our finances and whether I can support myself. I just want things to be separated fairly, and I want to stay in my home."

When I later met with Ervin, he showed signs of stress periodically, as he spoke about making mistakes in his marriage. "I realize that my marriage is over, and I know that it's mostly my fault. I don't want to get divorced, and I deeply regret the incident when I put my hands on Nusi."

"What troubles you most about getting divorced?"

Erwin began to fidget nervously with his hands. "I don't know how to live without my wife. And I'm lonely. I don't have anyone in my life but my wife and my kids and grandkids. I don't know how to take care of myself. And I never thought that I would be the type of person who would be divorced. I'm concerned about what others will think. And I know that I shouldn't have laid my hands on Nusi, but it's not all my fault. Did she tell you about the affair she had when our children were young? Did I leave her then? No. I wouldn't have even considered it. Marriage is forever, through good times and bad. But I've never really forgiven her for that, and I still think about it often."

"What result would you like to see from your divorce?"

"I'm concerned about how we can afford to live separately. I want to sell both the homes, and I want everything handled fairly for both of us. I'm hoping that I'll be able to move near my youngest daughter in Chicago so I can spend more time with my grandchildren."

After meeting with both of them, it was clear they were both emotionally and financially dependent on each other.

During the first teleconference, the financial neutral, Rebecca, expressed her concern. "Ervin and Nusi's financial situation is bleak. It worries me because Ervin was often confused during our meeting, particularly when discussing the finances."

I said, "Why don't I assess Ervin's and Nusi's readiness for the first collaborative team meeting in a joint meeting?"

The team agreed.

During my meeting with them, Ervin and Nusi said they understood what to expect at the first meeting. We covered the rules and communication guidelines without difficulty. However, as we went over each other's financial goals for the divorce, Ervin became disoriented and confused. He allowed me to contact his doctor to schedule a medical evaluation, and Nusi made plans to take him to his appointment. I also recommended that their daughter attend the collaborative team meeting, but they both refused. Neither of them wanted to "burden their children with their issues."

After Ervin's medical evaluation, the doctor cleared him to make his own decisions. As we got to know them better, it became evident they would need a lot of creativity to manage their limited finances and to successfully divorce. Because of her apparent involvement in their day-to-day lives, but also because of her familiarity with both English and Slovak, with the latter of which both clients were plainly more comfortable, we explored the possibility that they should include Jessica in their decision-making process. In the meantime, we scheduled the first team meeting.

During that meeting, we reviewed the process with them. The participation agreement, as well as a media release that our mentor requires for all *pro bono* collaborative matters, was reviewed and signed. Finances, as the main concern, were next on the agenda. Rebecca discussed the clients' assets and liabilities and provided everyone with documents. She explained, "Ervin and Nusi have exhausted their savings and are living solely on their monthly retirement checks."

Nusi added, "We each live frugally, and I have learned to be very resourceful."

The team reviewed their liabilities and made suggestions. We discussed questions about the property taxes and insurance for both homes. Rebecca had a suggestion. "The home that Ervin lives in has his insurance and taxes paid by escrow, but the home Nusi resides in no longer has a mortgage. Perhaps they would like to obtain a reverse mortgage for the home where Nusi lives?"

Nusi's attorney said, "I know a mortgage professional who can discuss a reverse mortgage with them." After the meeting, the clients met with the professional to discuss the reverse mortgage. After some thought, Nusi declined the option as she felt that she really did not fully understand it and did not feel comfortable pursuing it.

We needed to divide their assets, but getting a value for the two homes was a challenge because they had no money to pay for a property appraiser. The team brainstormed how we could get a *pro bono* assessment. In the end, the financial neutral found a real estate broker who would give us two "broker's price opinions" for free.

Next, we discussed how to make the upcoming tax and insurance payments, which were due in a few months.

Lastly, they were asked to bring in financial documents pertaining to their debts.

While wrapping up the meeting, the team strongly suggested that the clients bring Jessica to the next meeting, or at the very least, allow me to contact her. We had concerns about the language barrier, as well as Ervin's mental state, and hoped that she could help us ensure that he was thinking clearly and would not regret any choices he might make. They agreed to think about it.

After the first team meeting, the professionals realized just how dependent Ervin and Nusi were on each other, despite being separated for the past year. After 46 years together, there were roles and tasks for which each of them were responsible, and neither one knew how to perform the other's role.

The team worked hard to keep them both on task with their homework assignments. In addition, each of them was referred to many resources in the community to help them become more independent.

In the meantime, we continued to discuss whether getting Jessica involved would be helpful to getting this couple through their divorce process. During one of my phone calls to Nusi, she disclosed that the reason she did not want to directly involve her daughter was because she did not want to cause conflict between Jessica and her husband; it was "looked down upon to divorce in our culture."

The second teleconference consisted of the financial neutral giving the rest of the professionals an update on Ervin and Nusi's finances. Their assets consisted of the two homes. Because the broker's opinions of value were going to be done for free, it would take some time to have them completed. The team strategized ways to help them both understand the importance of having their daughter involved in the decision-making process. We addressed eldercare issues, and I filled everyone in on the various resources to which each client was referred, including which ones they were currently receiving, as well as those that would be put in place after the dissolution of marriage.

The goals for the second team meeting were to address ways that Ervin and Nusi could save some money each month and to provide them with a clear understanding of their probable finances. The financial neutral explained to them what their monthly income and debts would look like. They were each given a simple breakdown to help them understand their financial futures.

The professionals were all concerned by the breakdown and we discussed it at length. Regardless, Ervin and Nusi both expressed understanding. Nusi was determined to pursue the divorce, even though her financial future would be poverty-stricken. She would always tell us "I will find ways to make ends meet," and she would;

she was extraordinarily resourceful.

At the post-team meeting with the professionals, we began discussing various ways we could help improve their future outcome. Our mentor reminded us that we were only required to help them get divorced. We all looked at each other and agreed—it was not enough for this multi-disciplinary group. We were committed to helping this couple as much as possible and convincing them of the importance of including Jessica in their discussions.

At the third teleconference, the team discussed the value opinions that we received by email. There were some concerns about the values of the homes and how the clients, particularly Ervin, would perceive these numbers. Because discussing financial matters was a trigger for him, his lead counsel wanted to have a meeting with him prior to the next team meeting. His initial goal was to sell both homes. The team was not sure how he would handle selling his home while Nusi remained in the marital home.

There was a lot of tension in the third team meeting, but the professional team was prepared for it because the clients were getting down to the nitty-gritty. This meeting was the first one that they drove to separately because they were angry with each other.

With an incident of a domestic assault in their history, we took extra precautions before, during, and after the meeting. During the introduction, we again strongly suggested having one of their children involved in the process because of Ervin's history of getting confused, the increased stressfulness of the process, and the language barrier.

The financial neutral explained the appraisals for each home and presented some creative ways to equalize the payments. The attorneys concurred. In the end, both clients agreed to sell Ervin's home, but they were not in agreement as to what to do with the marital home. Ervin wanted it sold, and Nusi wanted to keep it. We told them again that we were not comfortable having either of them sign the legal documents without their daughter present and fully aware of the dissolution of marriage.

After much discussion, they finally agreed to allow me to contact their oldest daughter and to discuss the divorce process with her. The team decided to end the meeting early, as both clients were stressed, and to wait for me to contact Jessica.

Upon speaking to her, we learned that Ervin and Nusi never fought in front of their children, which extended into their adult lives. In fact, Jessica and both of her siblings were in denial about the divorce because their parents acted as if they were still together, even while they were separated.

After educating Jessica about the collaborative divorce process and explaining where her parents were in it, she agreed to talk to them about the marital home. She also agreed to attend the final meeting, as long as she was not asked to make decisions for or against either parent regarding the divorce.

In addition, she agreed to explain the situation to both of her siblings so that they, too, were up to speed, and understood the needs and goals of their parents.

It took four months from start to finish, but Ervin finally agreed to allow Nusi to stay in the marital home with certain restrictions that were added to the marital settlement agreement. Jessica came to the final team meeting and witnessed her parents signing the legal documents to dissolve their marriage. Although both of our clients verbalized understanding of the documents explained by the attorneys, it was plain to us all that Jessica played an integral role in assuring that both of her parents understood the ramifications of the agreement that they wanted to make, discussing the terms in Slovak with them both in front of us all for quite some time.

Her presence also had the beneficial effect on both Nusi and Ervin of calming them and allowing them to think more lucidly.

With their child's help, Nusi and Ervin successfully concluded their collaborative divorce.

Diane Rodriguez is a licensed clinical social worker, Florida Supreme Court certified family mediator, and a collaborative divorce neutral facilitator. She is also the founder of Guided Resolutions, a counseling and mediation service that specializes in helping individuals cope with life stressors and divorce amicably.

Ms. Rodriguez received a bachelor's degree in child development and family studies and her master's degree in clinical social work from Florida State University.

Her early years consisted of assessing and providing needs for children and their families, as well as assisting veterans and their families who were experiencing medical and/or mental health issues.

Ms. Rodriguez took some time off to raise her family and to return to college to earn a graduate certificate in conflict resolution. She is passionate about helping individuals resolve their differences respectfully, in addition to helping them gain insight into the trauma and lifelong consequences children involved in high-conflict divorce experience.

Ms. Rodriguez devotes her time volunteering at Selah Freedom, an organization that exists to end human trafficking and bring freedom to the exploited. She also facilitates a self-esteem/self-worth group for female inmates at the county jail.

Ms. Rodriguez feels honored to have had the privilege of having Joryn Jenkins mentor her in the first *pro bono* collaborative divorce matter resolved in Manatee County, Florida. You can reach her at Diane@GuidedResolutions.com.

As ardent peacemakers, we would like all matters to be resolved collaboratively. But sometimes, that is not appropriate. While every family could benefit from the collaborative process because of what it teaches about communication and co-parenting, if that family can reach a similar resolution with a less expensive process option, then the collaborative choice should not be forced upon them. Many spouses are able to sit maturely at the kitchen table and resolve their matters completely, or with just the help of an attorney to draft an agreement or to negotiate a few simple matters. A family of modest means may find itself in a worse condition if it chooses collaborative divorce because its limited assets may be consumed in just one or two full team meetings. If this causes negative feelings about the process that the family then shares, it certainly does not help our goal of spreading the collaborative word in a positive way.

Collaborative divorce may also be inappropriate for families in which a spouse suffers from addiction or mental health issues, there is domestic violence, or a spouse wants his day in court and to "win" while the other spouse "loses." These families should not be uniformly denied the collaborative process, but rather, should be more closely evaluated, usually by the mental health professional, to determine whether collaborative is an appropriate (and, perhaps, the best option) for them.

As professionals, we must help guide our clients to the best process option for them, even if it is not collaborative. – Ed. Note

DETERMINING THE SUITABILITY OF A DIVORCE FOR THE COLLABORATIVE PROCESS: AN ETHICAL RESPONSIBILITY
BY LORI SKIPPER, ESQ.

We all know now that collaborative is a kinder, gentler way to get divorced. But is it right for every family?

It can be tempting to try to fit every client into the collaborative model because it benefits so many. Who wouldn't want to improve their communication skills? To co-parent children better? To reach a resolution that considers a client's most important goals and interests?

As practitioners, we want more collaborative work on our resumes. With more of these matters under our belts, we can better market the process to new clients. In addition, we will connect with other collaborative professionals as we work on teams. But for some families, this process would be a disservice.

Families with fewer issues who work well enough together don't necessarily need a full team to help. In these cases, it is simply unethical to push the collaborative model. Individuals forced to take this approach may come away with negative feelings despite a good agreement if they could have reached the same end result for far less money. This is an ineffective way to market the collaborative approach.

Attorneys have a duty to explain every divorce process option to potential clients. Those choices include default divorce, kitchen table divorce, one lawyer drafting the spouses' agreement, one lawyer negotiating with the other spouse, mediation, cooperation, collaboration, and litigation. During consults, I go over each one.

My passion for collaborative practice shines through, and often, that means that my clients choose this option. However, sometimes, after hearing a consult's story, I suggest a different process. Really listening to clients means you'll be likely to suggest the best option for each one.

Often, collaborative is the best, but sometimes, it is not. For it to be successful in our community, we must recommend it for the right families—not all families—so that they have positive, cost-effective experiences. These are a couple of my experiences.

FRANK'S DIVORCE

I met with Frank on a Monday morning. We scheduled an early time before his long day as an auto mechanic. When I suggested breakfast at the Denny's near his job, he seemed grateful.

CHAMPIONS OF COLLABORATIVE DIVORCE

"I've never been to a lawyer's office, and I was nervous about it. I eat at Denny's every morning before work, so this is great!"

I arrived before he did and ordered coffee. As soon as he walked in, I recognized him, though I had never met him. I'd like to claim it was my remarkable power of perception, but his work shirt had his name embroidered on the front.

A large man with a dark complexion, he had muscular, furry arms and enormous hands. I could tell that he had scrubbed hard, but a layer of oil and grime remained beneath his nails and in the deep wrinkles of his hands. At first, his size made him seem intimidating, but as soon as he saw me rise, he broke into a warm smile that reached from ear-to-ear.

He shook my hand and drew me into a bear hug. "Attorney Skipper, thank you so much for your time and for meeting me at my favorite breakfast spot."

I dismissed the formalities. "Please, call me Lori. It's a pleasure to meet you."

After we ordered breakfast, a fruit bowl for me, a lumberjack special for him, we discussed why he wanted to retain me.

"I'm almost embarrassed to say this, but I've been married for almost ten years, and I don't even know where my wife is."

"Don't be embarrassed. I hear stories like this far more than you'd imagine. When was the last time you had contact with her?"

"Almost nine years now. I met Amber when we were both vacationing in Panama City. We had a whirlwind romance, spending every moment together after we met on the beach during the first hours of each of our vacations. I lived near Tampa at the time, but she lived in Alabama. When we reached the end of our vacations, we just couldn't bear to be apart, so she quit her job and moved into my home. Everything was great for a couple of months, so we got married at the courthouse. Young love, you know?"

I smiled, shaking my head, "Then what happened?"

"Once we got to know each other, we realized how different we were. After about a year of constant bickering or ignoring each other, I came home from work one day and she was gone with all of her stuff. She didn't leave a note or anything. It was kind of a relief, so I didn't even try to find her. I figured I'd deal with a divorce later."

"Understandable."

"And life got away from me as the years went by."

"What makes you want the divorce now?"

He smiled with warmth. "I met a wonderful woman. I believe I'm older and wiser now, and I really think she's the one. But I can't move ahead with her until I get a divorce. I wanted to take care of it on my own, without hiring an attorney, so I filled out all of the paperwork, but then I couldn't find Amber to serve her. I don't think that she'll object. She may not even respond, but I just need help getting it finished."

"I understand. It sounds like you're ready to take care of the past and start a new life."

"Exactly. So what do I do?"

My first thought, as always, was how to make this a collaborative matter. "Let me ask you a few questions. Did you have a child with Amber?"

"No."

"And you're sure that she wasn't pregnant when she left?"

"Well, I can't be completely certain, but I know that right before she took off, we went to a friend's party, and she got really drunk. She wouldn't have done that if she knew she was pregnant."

"Okay. Did you buy any assets or incur any liabilities when you were still together?"

"No. I owned my home and she just moved into it. We each had our own vehicles and our own credit cards. We tried to keep everything separate. We never even opened a bank account together."

"That certainly makes things easier. Technically, until you petition for divorce, any assets either of you acquires or liabilities either of you incurs are marital and could be split equally. But, since you kept everything so separate and have been living apart for so long, I suggest that you offer that you each keep what you have, and just finalize the divorce."

"That's what I was thinking, too, but I didn't know that I could be responsible for half of her debts." He looked worried. "I better get my petition filed quickly."

"That's a good idea. Let me tell you about your divorce options. We'll do a search for her, and if we can't find her, we'll have her served through publication. You said that she may not even respond once she receives your petition. She'll have 20 days to respond once she's served, but if she doesn't, we'll move for a default divorce."

"What does that mean? It sounds pretty technical."

"Actually, it would be the easiest, best case scenario. If she doesn't answer in the set time, we'll move for default. If she doesn't respond to that, the judge will eventually grant you what you requested in your divorce petition and finalize your divorce."

"That would be great. But what if she does respond?"

"Well, she may respond and agree to everything you requested. In that case, the judge will finalize your divorce with a simple hearing. Or, she may want to negotiate a bit without hiring her own attorney. I can talk with her directly if she doesn't have her own attorney, as long as she understands that I represent you and not her.

"She may decide to hire an attorney. If so, I can try to negotiate directly with her attorney without any formal processes. Because you don't have children, marital assets, or liabilities, I'd probably be able to get everything resolved by negotiating with her or her attorney."

"All of those options sound great. Are there others?"

"Yes. If we aren't able to work out an agreement with her or her attorney, we could attend mediation, which is where we all meet with a neutral professional who helps you to come to a fair agreement."

"That sounds expensive. I hope that it doesn't come to that. I only have about a thousand dollars for legal fees and we really don't have anything to fight over."

"I agree. Because of your situation and your limited funds, I think that mediation should be unnecessary, but I want to make you aware of all of your options. There's also cooperative divorce during which attorneys work together with other professionals to help you resolve your matters. And collaborative divorce is similar, but the attorneys and clients sign an agreement saying that the attorneys will disqualify themselves if the clients can't reach an agreement and have to litigate."

Frank interrupted, "Those sound like great options for people with more issues than we have, but I don't think that any of that will be necessary. And I don't have the money to pay all of those professionals."

"I totally understand. Although collaborative and cooperative divorce are great options for many divorcing families, they're not for everyone. Personally, I wish that everyone could afford a collaborative divorce. In even the simplest of situations, it can help because of the lessons that can be learned from each professional on the team. But that's just not the reality for many people."

Frank agreed, "Those plans sound like they'd be great for families with children and homes. My parents got divorced when I was ten, and they ended up hating each other. They had to go to court. I thought that was what everyone had to do."

"That leads me to the last option. Some families have to litigate their divorces in the courtroom. But, often, a litigated divorce completely ruins a couple's already fragile relationship. That can be catastrophic when children are involved. Litigated divorces are also expensive, and the people don't learn anything from them. I try to encourage my clients to avoid litigating their divorces, if possible. But unfortunately, sometimes litigation is necessary."

At this point, we had finished eating, and I paid the bill.

Frank said, "Thank you for breakfast and for all of the information. I think that we should use one of the first options you mentioned, but it's good to know what my other choices are. I have a friend who may want to talk to you about a collaborative divorce. She has two young children, and her husband is a doctor, so I'm sure they have some property to fight over. I'll give her your information."

"I'd appreciate that," I said as we exited the restaurant. Although I was disappointed collaborative didn't sound like a good choice for Frank, I was hopeful that his friend would get in touch with me and be the perfect candidate for it.

ANNIE'S DIVORCE

A few days later his friend, Annie, called. "My mechanic, Frank, gave me your name. I need to talk to you about a divorce, but I'm so scared that it's going to be a nightmare. When can I meet you?" We set a time for the next afternoon.

When she walked into my office, she had a blank, shell-shocked expression. She was not short, but she had a frailty that made her look extremely petite. Her long, highlighted blond hair resisted her attempts to style it and hung limply around her tired face. She wore a short-sleeved smock dress, and when she moved her arm, I could see a faint black-and-blue thumb mark on her upper arm.

"Tell me what brings you here, Annie."

"I'm at my wit's end. I've been married to Ben for 15 years, and I love him, but he's getting worse and worse. He's a doctor, and he works really long hours. He's always stressed, and when he comes home from work, he drinks a lot. When he sticks to wine, he's usually fine, but when he brings out the whiskey, I know it's going to be a long night."

I could see tears in her eyes. I handed her the tissue box. "What do you mean by that?"

She looked at her hands, kneading the tissue. "Ben gets angry and aggressive with me. He's always been like that, but lately, it's getting worse. He just got a promotion, so his job has been extra stressful. He used to just yell at me and call me horrible names, but last week, he grabbed me really hard and threw me against the wall."

As she looked up, a tear rolled down her face. "My girls are eight and ten. I can't have them seeing him verbally and physically abuse me."

"Did you file an injunction for protection against him?"

She hunched slightly and shook her head. "I couldn't. I thought it could make matters worse. And he works with children a lot, so I don't want it to affect his job. I just know that I want out."

As she told her story, I thought about how much this family could benefit from a collaborative team. A mental health professional could help address the power and control issues involved with domestic violence, as well as any other issues related to Ben's possible alcoholism.

However, I'd heard that divorces involving domestic violence and mental health issues may not be appropriate for collaborative divorce. Nevertheless, this still seemed to be the best option for them. I would give this some serious thought and talk to other collaborative colleagues and get their opinions.

I explained the various process options to Annie.

"I really think that collaborative would be perfect for us. I hope he'll agree to it."

We decided to take a week to each do some homework and determine at that point how we would proceed.

I immediately called my good friend who had been working as a collaborative coach for years. "I really want to help this woman, and I think that the entire family could benefit from our support, but there are definitely some domestic violence issues and possibly some alcoholism. I've always heard that those matters may not be appropriate for collaborative." I explained the general details of the situation. "What do you think?"

Susan said, "You're right that we have to be extra cautious when recommending collaboration to clients with issues like your client's. But I agree that litigation isn't the right choice for a couple like this. The stress and hostility they'd experience would likely be devastating. On the other hand, a strong collaborative team who is mindful of their issues could really help.

"The entire team needs to be alert to any subtle control Ben may use to try to influence Annie. Additionally, it may be helpful for him to agree to rehab before we begin. Most importantly, though, he needs to be open to the collaborative process. Has he retained an attorney yet?"

"Yes. Carl Rodriguez. I've worked with him in the past in both litigation and collaboration. He's a talented litigator, but since he's 'drunk the collaborative Kool-Aid,' I've really enjoyed working with him on collaborative matters. I was so relieved when he contacted me to say that he had been retained."

"How did he feel about the matter being collaborative?"

"He had the same reservations I did but was open to it. He'd explained it to his client as an option, and his client wasn't completely opposed."

"Would you mind," Susan asked, "if I called Carl to discuss this? I think that if we're all on the same page, we can really help this family. I'd like to go over the possibility of rehab with Carl, as well as making sure that his client is able to proceed collaboratively. He needs to be open to the process, and not just want his day in court, revenge, or to win while Annie loses. If Ben is agreeable, we should try to move forward."

"That would be great. Let me know what you find out."

A couple of days later, Susan called. She had spoken with Carl, and he believed that Ben was open to collaborative and had the right mindset to be successful. I was so relieved.

Once he'd completed a 30-day rehab for his alcoholism, we began the collaborative process. In just three months, they came to a complete agreement that was equitable, fair, and met their most important goals and interests. It was truly a testament to how a strong team can make a difference in a family, even in those with more complex issues like violence and addiction. I can only imagine what could have happened if this family had litigated. Thankfully, they opted for a kinder, gentler way.

When a divorce is appropriate for collaborative, magic can happen. The professionals must understand when—and when not—to encourage clients to proceed collaboratively.

Ms. Skipper received her Juris Doctor and graduated with honors from the University of Florida Levin College of Law in December 2004. As a law student member of the Virgil B. Hawkins Civil Clinic, Ms. Skipper assisted indigent clients with family law issues. She also received the Estates and Trusts Certificate for her intensive coursework in that practice area.

Ms. Skipper began working as an associate for Joryn Jenkins & Associates (n/k/a Open Palm Law) in April 2005. She is a Florida Supreme Court certified family law mediator, as well as a parenting coordinator. She has attended extensive introductory and advanced trainings in collaborative practice, participated in numerous collaborative matters, and assisted Joryn Jenkins in writing several of her books on collaborative practice.

In February 2015, Ms. Skipper had her first child, Tripp. She now works from home, juggling her career and parenthood. She spends her mornings teaching new mommies how to stay fit as a Fit4Mom fitness instructor and her afternoons continuing to practice law. She works hourly as an independent contractor for several attorneys. Somehow, she finds time to continue her passion for long-distance running. She recently qualified for the Boston Marathon and was the second overall female in the *Marathon of the Treasure Coast* with a time of 3:32:03.

Ms. Skipper has always gravitated towards alternative dispute resolution for families in conflict, and she is especially enthusiastic about the benefits of collaborative practice, for both her clients and herself.

Ms. Skipper can be contacted at LSkipper5@TampaBay.rr.com.

Asperger's Disorder is an autism spectrum disorder considered to be on the "high functioning" end of the spectrum. Affected children and adults have difficulty with social interactions and exhibit a restricted range of interests and/or repetitive behaviors.

According to Autism Society, diagnosis of Asperger's Disorder has increased in recent years, although it is unclear whether it is more prevalent or more professionals are detecting it. According to the Center for Disease Control and Prevention, about one in 68 children has been identified with autism spectrum disorder (ASD). Among those with ASD, it is 4.5 times more common among males than among females.

Considering these percentages, chances are good that, at some point, you will encounter a client with Asperger's. You may wonder whether the collaborative process is the appropriate divorce process option for these folks. With the help of the mental health professional, the team can better understand the needs of a client with Asperger's Disorder and craft settlement agreements that complement his or her attributes. – Ed. Note

ASPERGER'S DISORDER AND THE COLLABORATIVE PROCESS: HOW TO BEST HELP YOUR CLIENT
BY STEPHANIE MOULTON SARKIS, PhD, NCC, LMHC

Jane and her husband, Sam, are divorcing via the collaborative process. They have one child, Susie, who is a year old. You've noticed Jane doesn't make much eye contact when she is asked questions by the collaborative team. She also has been looking down at her phone for quite a bit of the meeting. When the team began discussing the division of assets, Jane stated that she is adamant about staying in the family home – even though, at her current income, this would be difficult. When other living arrangements are presented, Jane becomes flustered and repeats that she is staying in the house. It appears that she will not entertain any other options. When Sam comments that Jane can't be a stay-at-home mother anymore, Jane shuts down and looks defeated. From that point on, Jane doesn't speak except when asked a direct question. At one point, Jane says "I need to leave right now", and exits the room. You follow her out and find her in tears in the lobby. When you ask her how you can help, she says, "It's just too much. Too much change. Just too much."

In this scenario, Jane was previously diagnosed with Asperger's Disorder. Asperger's is a high-functioning form of autism. This means that, unless you were in a social situation with Jane, you might not even notice that she has a disorder. Difficulty with social skills, communication, and coping with change are hallmark traits of Asperger's. People with Asperger's can live productive, happy lives – they may just need more support than others.

If a parent with Asperger's must go back into the work force after being a stay-at-home parent, it can cause a feeling of sheer terror for her. At home, it was just her and the kids during the day - she knew where everything was, she knew what to expect – it was safe. Now she is fearful about having to do job interviews, working with people – it is all just too much. The fear can be paralyzing. Sometimes you will find people with Asperger's in protracted legal cases because to finalize the divorce would be one of the biggest changes they've ever had to deal with – and that is just unthinkable.

Throughout this chapter, when the term "Asperger's Disorder" is used, it is referring to what is now known in the American Psychiatric Association's *Diagnostic and Statistical Manual of Mental Disorders* (5th ed., 2013) as Autism Spectrum Disorder, Level 1. The public is more familiar with the term Asperger's Disorder. This is a high-functioning type of autism spectrum disorder, where a person has difficulties with social interaction and nonverbal communication, has awkward mannerisms, has difficulty understanding abstract statements, and difficulty maintaining eye contact. People with Asperger's Disorder are very individual, in that they can display different variations of symptoms.

Collaborative law provides a more productive atmosphere for people with Asperger's, and creates much less stress than appearing in court. People with Asperger's may not make effective witnesses because they may inadvertently skip key parts of testimony or "shut down" on the stand due to a feeling of panic. Clients with Asperger's may mistakenly appear to be unemotional or unattached to their child or children – and in litigation, opposing counsel may use this to portray your client as lacking empathy towards her child. However, people with Asperger's can be excellent parents - in fact, they tend to be even more attentive to their children than people without Asperger's. Next you will learn some common challenges and solutions when working with a client with Asperger's.

Challenge: Your client has difficulty understanding metaphors, sayings, or multistep recommendations.

Solution: Speak in concrete terms, and avoid the use of metaphor and sayings. If you catch yourself using a turn of phrase, quickly add, "what I am meaning to say is...." Ask for a client to paraphrase what you have recommended, in order to make sure you were understood correctly. Write all instructions down for your client.

Challenge: Your client has difficulty accepting change, or being flexible on plans. "Brainstorming" for solutions is very difficult for your client. Divorce is one of the biggest life changes anyone can go through – and for a person with Asperger's, that stress is multiplied. You may find clients that refuse to leave the marital home, even though with their current income and child support they could not afford to do so; clients that may refuse to give up a particular asset for which you cannot find a logical reason for the refusal; or unwillingness to change a drop-off/pick-up plan – "it has to be at 3pm."

Solution: Acknowledge the difficulty of accepting change. Vocational support services are essential if your client is reentering the work force. Your client's fears about employment are justified - people with Asperger's are going to have more difficulties being hired than people who don't have it (Baldwin, Costley, and Warren,

2014). Vocational Rehabilitation (VR) can provide a case worker and a job coach, if your client qualifies (Chappel and Somers, 2010). VR staff can help your client find a job that increases her chances of success. Jobs that can be best for people with Asperger's are those with a structured, predictable schedule and where expectations and responsibilities are clear. The best workplace for a person with Asperger's is one with as few "unwritten rules" as possible.

Challenge: Your client has difficulty interacting with others, and makes very limited eye contact. In the United States, the majority culture encourages direct eye contact as a sign of attention and honesty.

Solution: Holding eye contact is overwhelming for a person with Asperger's. Know that even if a person with Asperger's is not making direct eye contact with you, they are listening to you. If you feel that your client tuned out during a collaborative meeting, call for a break and take your client aside and make sure they are understanding what is being talked about.

Challenge: Your client becomes overwhelmed easily when there are more than a few people in the conference room, or if your office phone rings often. When your client gets overwhelmed, she tends to hyper focus on her phone or tablet. Repetitive noise, especially high-pitched noise, can cause people with Asperger's to become very uncomfortable and feel a sense of needing to "flee." Also, being "put on the spot" can cause your client to go into "fight or flight" mode.

Solution: Put phones and other electronic devices in silent mode. Make your office and conference room as hospitable as possible. Avoid direct overhead lighting, especially fluorescent lights. The buzzing from fluorescent lights can be overwhelming for people with Asperger's. Use indirect light, like lamps, instead. Use a white noise machine to block out extraneous noise. Take frequent established breaks – every 30 minutes is recommended. Know what cues to look for when your client is overwhelmed. Talk with your client ahead of time to ask them how to best know when they are feeling overwhelmed. If your client says they aren't sure, note that this is common for people with Asperger's to be unaware of when they are approaching panic. Attorneys and clients can work out a nonverbal signal between them so the client can tell the attorney quietly that they need to take a break. Examples of nonverbal signals that have been used are the client scratching her head or tugging on her earlobe.

Challenge: Your client displays what you perceive as a lack of emotion and empathy when interacting with others; her facial expressions are limited, and her voice tone tends not to change. She also appears to be detached when talking about her children. Some of the staff in your office have told you your client seems "cold." Your client also has difficulty "reading" your facial expressions and your body language. When you call your client, they usually text or email back.

Solution: Nonverbal communication is 90% of communication – and it is very difficult for people with Asperger's to process this information. In addition, people with Asperger's can be very attached to their children, but just have difficulties communicating that to others. Difficulty communicating, especially communicating about emotions, is difficult for people with Asperger's. To many people with Asperger's, the social art of small talk is difficult to comprehend. Do not take it personally if your client doesn't appear to engage in pleasantries at the beginning of a meeting – he is more likely to say hello, then immediately sit down at the conference table, unpack, and set up their workspace. In addition, talking on the phone causes a great deal of stress. People with Asperger's do want social contact – they just aren't sure how to go about doing it. This leads to feelings of isolation (Koegel, et al. 2013).

Rarely is a person with Asperger's trying to upset you, ignore you, or appear unfeeling – in fact, the last thing he wants to do is upset you. If you find yourself getting frustrated by your client, ask yourself why. Is it something your client did or said? While having Asperger's does not excuse behavior, it does give you an idea of why a behavior occurred. Also remember that there is a difference between *won't* and *can't*. Many times, with Asperger's, the brain cannot process social subtleties or cues.

Challenge: Your client appears to be ruminating or obsessing on small details of his case, and can't see the "big picture" during collaborative meetings. Paying too much attention to detail and ruminating can be common when a person has Asperger's – and these symptoms intensify under stress. While paying attention to detail can be of benefit in some careers, like engineering, it can hinder progress in a collaborative setting. Your client may be very focused on their spouse doing the "right" thing – due to "black or white" thinking. For example, your client is very focused on one instance of not being offered first right of refusal to watch the children. When you try to change the subject, your client returns to that issue. In your client's case, his soon-to-be ex-wife was going to the store for just a couple of hours and asked her mother to watch the children. Your client points out that the parenting plan clearly says that he has right of first refusal.

Solution: People with Asperger's can have difficulty understanding the "gray areas" of situations. The agreement says what the agreement says - period. Parenting plans should provide very detailed guidelines – even more so than usual. Be very clear about areas of the parenting plan that are up to the parents to determine. Your client will view the parenting plan as an absolute, a document that must be followed and does not give leeway. If there are some areas where parents will be fluid in plans, try to limit these instances as much as possible, and detail in the parenting plan where this fluidity will occur. In the case of right of first refusal, consider using language in the parenting plan such as, "The other parent will have the right of refusal if the parent will be away from the children for 4 hours or more. When the mother will be out for less than three hours, the mother will ask the children's grandmother to watch the children.

Challenge: Your client wants to know the details of a collaborative meeting ahead of time – details that you find inconsequential. He is texting you late at night with questions.

Solution: People with Asperger's crave structure and "sameness." Try to meet on the same day of the week and time, as much as possible. Confirm all appointments the day before, preferably via text and email. on the phone can cause anxiety for people with Asperger's). Create clear, written agendas for collaborative meetings – and send them out a week ahead, if possible. The further ahead your client has this information, the better. In your client agreement, establish limits about your availability after hours. Also let your client know that their emails will be answered as soon as possible – and it may be a day or two before you are able to respond.

Challenge: Your client is experiencing is a great amount of stress and difficulty coping, and you feel you have done all that you can in order to make the collaborative process a less stressful one. Your client is having difficulty understanding the long-term consequences of decisions and the subtleties of negotiation.

Solution: Going through a divorce or other legal procedure is extremely stressful for anyone. If a client has Asperger's, the feeling of overwhelm can be paralyzing. Refer your client to a counselor that specializes in Asperger's/Autism Spectrum Disorders. Make sure your client has support in terms of friends and family. Having a support system is strongly correlated with increasing a person with Asperger's quality of life (Khanna, et al. 2014). Consider having a trusted friend or family member accompany your client to meetings. It may be possible that your client is not able to represent themselves fairly and adequately – both processing long-term consequences and understanding social subtleties can be impaired when your client has Asperger's. Consider your client's options and if the collaborative process is the right solution.

With your guidance and the collaborative process, your client with Asperger's can navigate a life-changing event with less trauma. This results in a better quality of life in the future – for your client, the co-parent, and their children.

References

American Psychiatric Association. (2013). *Diagnostic and statistical manual of mental disorders* (5th ed.). Arlington, VA: American Psychiatric Publishing.

Baldwin, S., Costley, D., & Warren, A. (2014). Employment activities and experiences of adults with high-functioning autism and Asperger's disorder. *Journal of Autism and Developmental Disorders*, *44*(10), 2440-2449.

Chappel, S. L., & Somers, B. C. (2010). Employing persons with autism spectrum disorders: A collaborative effort. *Journal of Vocational Rehabilitation*, *32*(2), 117-124.

Khanna, R., Jariwala-Parikh, K., West-Strum, D., & Mahabaleshwarkar, R. (2014). Health-related quality of life and its determinants among adults with autism. *Research in Autism Spectrum Disorders*, *8*(3), 157-167.

Koegel, L. K., Ashbaugh, K., Koegel, R. L., Detar, W. J., & Regester, A. (2013). Increasing socialization in adults with Asperger's syndrome. *Psychology in the Schools*, *50*(9), 899-909.

Stephanie Moulton Sarkis, Ph.D., NCC, LMHC, DCMHS is the bestselling author of five books: *10 Simple Solutions to Adult ADD: How to Overcome Chronic Distraction & Accomplish Your Goals*; *Natural Relief for Adult ADHD: Complementary Strategies for Increasing Focus, Attention, and Motivation With or Without Medication*; *Adult ADD: A Guide for the Newly Diagnosed*; *ADD and Your Money: A Guide to Personal Finance for Adults with Attention Deficit Disorder*; and *Making the Grade with ADD: A Student's Guide to Succeeding in College with Attention Deficit Disorder.*

Dr. Sarkis received her degrees and training from the University of Florida. She is an American Mental Health Counselors Association diplomat and clinical mental health specialist in child and adolescent counseling. Additionally, she is a Florida licensed mental health counselor and a national certified counselor. She is a Florida Supreme Court certified family and circuit civil mediator. Dr. Sarkis facilitates collaborative divorce and also is a parent coordinator.

She maintains a private practice in Tampa, Florida, where she counsels adults with attention deficit hyperactivity disorder (ADHD), autism spectrum disorder (including Asperger's), and anxiety.

Dr. Sarkis is a blogger for *Psychology Today* and *The Huffington Post*. She has been published numerous times, including in the *Journal of Attention Disorders*, the *National Psychologist*, and *The ADHD Report.*

Her website is www.StephanieSarkis.com, and she can be reached at Stephanie@StephanieSarkis.com.

According to The National Coalition Against Domestic Violence, *nearly 20 people are physically abused by an intimate partner in the United States every minute. During one year, that equates to more than ten million victims. One in three women and one in four men have been victims of some sort of physical violence by an intimate partner within their lifetimes.*

Domestic violence tends to worsen at the end of relationships, putting the victim and children in more danger, and often resulting in the victim opting to just stay in the relationship for fear of leaving. Therefore, it is crucial for the collaborative team to be alert to symptoms of domestic violence. Many victims will be afraid to mention it, so it is important to understand the signs that domestic violence is, or has, occurred.

In collaborative divorce, it is especially important for the professionals to be aware of silent power struggles between the victim and the aggressor, as well as intimidation by the aggressor. If an agreement is reached that seems unfair to the victim, the professionals should help the victim speak up, rather than just roll over and agree to an inequitable agreement.

While couples with a history of domestic violence are not always well suited for a collaborative divorce, with the help of the mental health professional and the rest of the professionals, many of these couples can resolve their matters collaboratively and learn skills that will help them going forward. – Ed. Note

DOMESTIC VIOLENCE AND COLLABORATIVE DIVORCE
BY LINDA M. PETERMAN, CRC, LMHC

Opinions vary in the collaborative world about whether collaborative divorce is the best choice when domestic violence is an issue. The decision, however, should be made on a case-by-case basis. The kind of violence and the circumstances of the distinct couple are key factors in the decision. Studies indicate that one-in-three to one-in-five divorces are a result of domestic violence. Therefore, when physical aggression is part of the relationship, this complicated issue must be addressed.

To determine how appropriate collaborative may be, evaluate these factors about the abuse—the type, the severity, and the emotional state of the victim. We must consider the definition of domestic violence, which varies depending upon the source.

TYPES OF DOMESTIC VIOLENCE

The Uniform Collaborative Law Act (UCLA) defines a "coercive or violent relationship" as one that is characterized by domestic violence as physical abuse, alone or in combination with sexual, economic, or emotional abuse, stalking, or other forms of coercive control by an intimate partner or household member, often for the purpose of establishing and maintaining power and control over the victim. The following are definitions of the different types of domestic violence:

1. *Coercion without violence* consists of verbal abuse, emotional abuse, sexual abuse, stalking, isolating, manipulating, blaming, making all the decisions, and many more controlling tactics. The perpetrator attempts to get what he wants with an implied, credible, negative threat and with consequences for noncompliance. Men usually use the victim's vulnerabilities to wear her down, invoke fear, and promote emotional dependency. If this works, abusers have no need to resort to physical violence. Some coercive words, actions, and gestures known only to the couple may be seen in collaborative meetings but will mean nothing to the team.

2. *Coercion with violence* combines emotional manipulation with restraining, pushing, shoving, pulling hair, throwing things, destroying property, hitting, slapping, punching, or using a weapon.

3. *Violence without coercion* can be determined when you look at the purpose of the violence, as well as the impact of the behavior. Many times, relational conflict instigates the violence. This pattern, triggered by men and women, occurs in unhealthy relationships and precedes steps toward divorce. This may be a chronic pattern instigated by frustration, anger, or stress; an argument; the threat of separation or divorce; a crisis (financial, parenting, job, extended family, etc.); alcohol; and/or mental illness.

    However, these examples do not consist of an underlying pattern of power and control. They are fueled by anger, frustration, hurt, fear, or a change in brain chemistry which affects emotions and behavior. This is an important distinction that will be a large factor in determining whether or not a couple should proceed with a collaborative divorce process.

For the team to be effective, its members must be trained to recognize power and control tactics and learn how to stop them. Abusers are accustomed to getting their way through manipulation, threats, guilt trips, blame, minimization, and intimidation, and they will try to use these methods throughout the process. The mental health professional's insight and skill will help ensure that this does not occur.

WHY CHOOSE COLLABORATIVE?

Depending on the matter, the collaborative process can be the best choice for people in a domestic violence relationship. The process enables communication and understanding, as well as a win/win scenario. As a result, the team will protect the victim from pressure to agree or settle simply to end arguments and badgering.

The abuser may like the collaborative set up because he sees it as a way to exert power and control. He is also more likely to comply with an agreement he has made himself. Because it is voluntary and not court-ordered mediation or counseling, he may be more receptive. His responses may improve if he feels he is being listened to, treated fairly, and given clear expectations for future behavior. The privacy of collaborative practice may allow him to admit to abuse, seek help, or change.

HOW TO ACHIEVE COLLABORATIVE SUCCESS

Success will require both clients to hone their communication skills. The facilitator, coaches, or a counselor for both clients can help. Domestic violence matters are an ideal time to have a coach for each client. This gives the victim one more advocate to help her have a voice. Caucusing, or having the spouses in separate rooms with the professionals meeting with each one individually, may be necessary at times.

Some behaviors an abuser may exhibit must be addressed for a successful outcome. The professionals should assess the abuser's level of denial and need for control. If disrespectful, manipulative, threatening, blaming, deceitful, contemptuousness, and constantly interrupting, the team must intervene. Full disclosure is mandatory, and he or she may use secrecy and dishonesty to maintain control.

The victim may also have some detrimental behaviors. She may be afraid to disclose information such as plans, goals, interests, thoughts, ideas, and more. This blocks the necessary transparency, openness, honesty, and willingness to participate. Counseling for both clients before the full team meetings begin may be a viable and smart option.

Next, the victim's emotional concerns must be considered. Is the individual capable of participating in collaborative meetings with the abuser? A lawyer must not begin or continue a collaborative process unless requested to do so by the client, and then only if the lawyer "reasonably believes that the safety of the party or prospective party can be protected adequately during the process." (Uniform Collaborative Law Act, Section 15).

Informed consent is very important for a victim. She must understand collaborative practices and how they may impact her in the divorce process. Examples are collaborative guidelines and principles, the disqualification provision, the makeup of the professional teams, client decision-making and communication, voluntary disclosure of information, confidentiality, and the time and cost. The consequences of termination and disqualification for the victim must be discussed and considered.

Domestic violence victims are more likely to leave the relationship when the following has occurred:

- *She recognizes the cycle.* She realizes that things are not changing and, no matter what she does, the abuse will continue.
- *The abuse is affecting her children.* Mothers worry that their sons are behaving like their fathers, their daughters are getting the wrong messages, and children are acting out or voicing their concerns for Mom's safety or their own. Children grow tired of witnessing the abuse or being abused themselves.
- *She has a support system or other options are revealed.* When a victim receives additional support from family, friends, and outside sources and knows her legal rights, she may feel ready to leave an abusive relationship.
- *The positive reinforcement from the relationship is removed.* The honeymoon phase of the cycle of violence may fail; the charm and empty promises, gifts, and good times aren't enough. The negatives of the relationship outweigh whatever positives exist. When a victim achieves some financial independence, and has begun taking care of her emotional needs, she may gain the confidence to try to make it on her own. Sometimes the value system of the victim has changed. Her health, safety, and happiness and that of any children may become more important than having a two-parent family.

Many concerns and issues for victims parallel other divorces. However, financial abuse and control occur when a victim is dependent on money from her spouse to live in addition to being emotionally dependent on him. Abusers have been known to threaten to take away the children, to cut off financial support, to ruin the victim's reputation, and to cause them to lose their jobs and their relationships with extended family and friends. Other similar fears involve those of change, an unknown future, failure, loneliness, and embarrassment.

Collaborative practice requires the team to evaluate the people and characteristics of each divorce. Coping skills and resiliency differ from person to person. Some victims fight back, seek help, and are looking for a way out, ready to openly rebel against their abusers.

For example, if a traumatized victim has no children, but enough money, she may get an attorney and litigate in order to completely avoid her abuser and make a clean break.

However, litigation can be worse for a victim because of its adversarial makeup, which further perpetuates power and control by encouraging a win/lose scenario. The combative approach lets an abuser deny the abuse and have his attorney defend him. In litigation, a relationship with domestic violence will consist of filing harassing motions, seeking full custody of the children, making false allegations, and filing parallel actions.

When dealing with abusers, be aware that they may attempt to intimidate the entire team, refuse to make financial disclosures, enlist team members to pressure the victim to settle, and quit the process.

The collaborative process also brings fairness, balance, and equality, something missing from the relationship. The team can help prevent more abuse or accusations by having safety mechanisms in place. Attorneys, and especially mental health professionals, must determine a victim's ability to stand up for herself and negotiate. Sometimes, the victim needs counseling before she can do this. The process may give her some power that she has not had before. She has the opportunity to stand up for herself, express opinions, assume responsibility for herself, and solve problems. In other words, she can have a voice. Addressing emotional issues in a safe setting can benefit victims.

Separated women suffer higher rates of violence than married or divorced women. In fact, 70-75% of murders happen after victims have threatened to leave or have left the relationship. Therefore, it is important for the victim's attorney and the neutral facilitator to meet regularly with the client to check for immediate safety issues.

A safety plan is critical. Even without physical abuse, a victim may fear an abuser will exert more severe control as their relationship changes. The victim knows the abuser, so the team must encourage her to share this information that will help keep her safe. UCLA allows collaborative lawyers to seek or respond to emergency orders "to protect the health, safety, welfare, or interest" of parties or family and household members, as defined by the applicable state protective order statute. We must answer this question: "Can the victim provide full disclosure safely?"

A collaborative divorce provides both clients with a support system and a cooperative approach that offsets the unequal power balance. Victims gain empowerment—and an equal say. Although mutually beneficial resolutions will be challenging with abusive relationships, it can provide the victim better protection than litigation. Therefore, the collaborative divorce process *can* be appropriate for relationships in which domestic violence or abuse has occurred.

Linda Peterman is a licensed mental health counselor and certified rehabilitation counselor in Hillsborough County, Florida. She has worked in the field of domestic violence for the past 20 years as an expert witness, a board member of the Hillsborough County Domestic Violence Task Force, a speaker and trainer for various professional groups, and an advocate for domestic violence victims. She has authored several articles published in professional journals on domestic violence.

Ms. Peterman has served as a neutral facilitator in collaborative family matters since 2013. Her fellow collaborative team members appreciate her organization, attention to detail, rational thinking, and ability to keep meetings focused and on task.

Ms. Peterman served on the board of Next Generation Divorce for two years as the program coordinator. She contributed to the board by showing respect for each of her fellow board members, committing to being at every meeting, and educating the members on the role of the mental health professional in the collaborative process.

Ms. Peterman is also a Florida Supreme Court certified family mediator and a parent coordinator. Her private counseling practice focuses on helping people create and keep healthy intimate relationships and learn to recognize unhealthy ones. In addition, she conducts trainings and seminars on various topics including life's transitions, interpersonal communication, grief and loss, anxiety and depression, and other issues pertinent to emotional health and happiness.

Reach Ms. Peterman at LindaMPeterman@earthlink.net.

For those of us who wish to be full-time peacemakers, we must offer our services in creative ways (like unbundled services) and for more matters than just divorces. Helping couples negotiate prenuptial agreements is a great way to expand the collaborative services that you offer. Presumably, these couples are in love and looking at their futures optimistically. If we can organize a collaborative team of professionals for them at this time when they are hopeful and happy, we can teach them skills that will help them in their marriages. By teaching them how to better communicate before they even walk down the aisle, we set them up for a better chance of success in a lifelong marriage. When there are troubles during the marriage, they can reconvene their collaborative team to assist them, and hopefully, to rescue their marriage, if the problems have escalated to that degree. If their union ultimately crumbles, the collaborative team can reconvene once again to help them to decide on any issues that were not addressed in the prenuptial agreement, and, perhaps, to help them negotiate deviations from the agreement. – Ed. Note

NEGOTIATING PRENUPTIAL AGREEMENTS UTILIZING THE COLLABORATIVE PROCESS
BY BRENDA BAIETTO, ESQ.

Eight years ago, I became a family mediator and stopped litigating. Along with mediating, I was excited by and reading a lot about collaborative practice (CP). My mind "switch" was a key component to the overhaul of my practice. As a result of litigating for over 15 years, position-based argument was my primary style, despite a strong tendency in my family law cases to seek out problem-solving approaches. You see, with family matters, especially divorce, I quickly learned that if I could help the other client find reasonable satisfaction, my client would be happier and the family would function better moving forward. Seeing these results and more referrals, I did not ignore this urge. Over time and with continuing education and the practice of new negotiation skills, something amazing happened. I realized how much I value marriage and the family.

Marriage and family are the bedrock of society. I work to promote marriage. Divorce hurts families—social science tells us that. I empathize with spouses, children, and families going through divorce. Whether one spouse is hurt because she is being divorced or a spouse is truly suffering in a marriage, I am called to help in ways that promote marriage, preserve the family, help spouses learn and grow, and enable children to stay connected to their parents. So not only did my mindset change but I also began to see my counselor-at-law role as a privilege and a vocation. My role could include speaking with and offering potential clients processes that promoted better outcomes.

Explaining all of the divorce process options to a client is crucial. As the consult progresses, many times it becomes clear that the client would prefer a collaborative process for a variety of reasons. When children are involved, the family must still be protected despite the divorce. In addition, collaborative includes the opportunity to have a group of professionals working for the entire situation. Money for the divorce is invested more wisely, and each person is empowered to determine his or her own outcome.

My clients appreciate the fact that I connect my values to the collaborative process because they get an attorney who not only "practices" collaborative law but *is* collaborative and will work for the needs of the family. Not all consults whom I think should go collaborative do, however, how you talk about your values and how you talk about CP is meaningful to people and often causes them to reevaluate their situations.

I remember speaking with Raj for the first time on the telephone. Before I knew what the issue was, he had conferenced his fiancée Jen into the call. They were calling about a prenuptial agreement because they planned to elope the following month. Raj followed that statement with another bombshell.

"Brenda, we love one another so much. Jen is an independent

woman, and we have decided to keep everything separated, and that, should we divorce, there will be no alimony. That's the gist of it."

I waited, letting that statement hang in the air a bit.

Jen chimed in, "Oh yes, Raj is the most amazing man I have ever met, and our love is bigger than money, including alimony."

I offered them a process-only consult, explaining there would be no legal advice given. They agreed.

When I do joint consults, to be safe, I have the couple sign a waiver of potential conflict. Once that is out of the way, I begin on an optimistic note. For Raj and Jen, I focused on their love. I spent the first few minutes learning how they met and what brought them together. Asking them to elaborate on their relationship, they were eager to share the joy each brought to the other's life. An important piece that stood out to me was how Raj's divorce had really overshadowed their relationship from the outset.

Raj, a physician, was a conservative man from India in his mid-thirties.

Jen, an insurance specialist, was considerably younger and much more energetic. "Raj has been through a horrible three-year divorce. His ex is a monster and has taken every last penny for child support and alimony. Dealing with her nonstop for so long has truly been draining. I could never think of hurting him by trying to go after his money like she has. After all, I have my own job and my own home. I just want to be married and live happily ever after."

I smiled at her.

She continued as though she was describing a dream, "Being married to Raj is all I want. Love can take care of anything, Brenda."

I glanced at Raj who was holding her hand and smiling at me. I asked him to tell me about his divorce.

"I was married for ten years and have two kids. The relationship no longer worked, so I asked for a divorce. She fought me for everything; she didn't want me to have the kids. No amount of money was enough."

Jen said, "Her behavior is completely crazy. I've witnessed nearly all of the divorce and watched her purposefully hurt Raj and use the kids to hurt him." She had tears in her eyes.

I gave her a Kleenex.

Raj said, "I can't go through something like that again. I'm out of money; I have nothing left. Jen and I agreed we need something in writing to prevent that from happening again. We looked online and found this premarital agreement and wanted to see if you could help us draft it."

Jen said, "I have a lawyer cousin who'll look it over for me even though she isn't a prenup lawyer. But I probably won't even need her. I completely understand what I'm doing, so what happens next?"

Silence. They clearly needed more information about what a prenuptial agreement is and its ramifications. Moreover, their rush to marry on the heels of a last-minute agreement could wreak havoc on their relationship. Their haste could cause significant issues to the reliability of the agreement.

So I explained. "A prenuptial agreement is a negotiation. Usually, one person prepares the agreement with an attorney and dictates most of the terms. The other person's attorney reviews it so that person can decide what changes to make, if any. The back and forth process is often quite stressful as the couple becomes aware of the terms each one wants.

"If they eventually *do* divorce, prenuptial agreements may be challenged, and may not stand up. If a big discrepancy in the ability to bargain appears, a judge could find it unfair. Having an agreement drafted just weeks before the wedding could raise issues. The biggest concern, however, is that the person who receives the prenuptial agreement may fail to communicate her wants or needs, planting the seeds of distrust. This is like poisoning the marriage from the start."

They looked dejected. Each of them fidgeted in their seats.

Jen leaned in, "We absolutely do not want that! I love this man, and I know he loves me. We know exactly what we want in this agreement."

I continued, "These negotiations are usually confrontational even if you're certain about what you want, because of the back and forth between attorneys in order to establish the details.

"Because you want to get married in a month and have yet to set the terms, your stress will increase. This will negatively affect the most beautiful thing you two have: a love that seeks a permanent commitment."

He looked at her. "Jen, I love you. You know that. We made an agreement—no alimony, right?"

She nodded.

I took a minute to remind them of the importance of marriage and the family. As I delved into the beauty of marriage, the permanence, the vows, the love . . . .

Jen said to Raj, "Honey, we have come up with what we're keeping separate, but what are we going to share?"

He was visibly uncomfortable. "We agreed to do this!"

Jen looked at Raj for a minute. I could see the wheels turning in her brain.

I broke the silence. "You two have some things to figure out and that's fine. Raj, your concern about your future and money is okay and reasonable. But, Jen, right now you have more questions and that is okay and reasonable. I expected this. It's a good thing."

Raj said to Jen, "We know we want kids. We know we want to live in your house. If we make additions to your house, does it become ours?"

Jen looked at me.

"Great questions. As you think about this more, you'll probably have other questions." I moved into explaining a collaborative process. "It sounds to me like you want to work out these questions together."

"Oh, yes!" they said in unison, their faces brightening.

I continued, "Let me explain how the collaborative process is used to prepare a prenuptial agreement. We eliminate the ping-pong sort of exchange. You each have an attorney, but all of you plan the agreement together in a series of respectful and efficient meetings, designed to reach fair solutions. Most importantly, with a process based on open communication, the risk of later invalidation is reduced.

"Collaboratively-trained attorneys promote their client's interests but problem solve together. In your case, you might also hire a neutral financial professional. He would help you exchange financial information and educate you about monetary options. Rather than a hostile process, the collaborative environment is safe and supportive and guided by professionals."

"But I don't need an attorney," Jen said. "I have one, and Raj trusts her too, even though she's a personal injury attorney."

"I'd be happy to talk to her about a collaborative process." I told Jen about my local collaborative group. Some of the professionals not only specialized in preparing prenuptial agreements but also embraced the collaborative process.

Raj seemed concerned. I asked him, "What's bothering you?"

"This is going to be expensive, and I've just been through the ringer with my divorce. I don't know if I can afford it." He sighed.

"You will pay the hourly rates of three professionals. However, that's a small investment to maximize the chances that this agreement won't be invalidated. Sounds to me like this is important to both of you, and for that reason alone, it deserves to be treated that way.

"Raj, Jen, you came in glowing with love for each other. You're talking about getting married, married in your faith, married before your community, married with vows to one another.

"If you both really believe that this agreement is best for your relationship, collaborating on it with professional help is the surest way of keeping that love alive and not tainting it with an ugly process that offers you less security about the agreement itself. You understand this precisely because of how difficult Raj's divorce has been."

"Did I tell you she's appealing?" Raj interjected.

"Nope. Perhaps that's something else to consider."

After a half hour, Jen asked me to follow up with a letter explaining the process "just as I had done today." She wanted directions to my collaborative group website and the name of some attorneys I could recommend so she could show the information to her parents. She wanted to be an equal paying part and knew her parents would appreciate the process.

A week later, Raj called, thanking me for my follow-up letter to Jen and letting me know her parents were pleasantly surprised to learn about the collaborative process. They were ready and willing to help. I expected the case to move forward.

But then Raj said, "I've decided not to get married yet."

I am pretty certain my mouth dropped open.

"I'm going to wait. I'm barely out of my divorce, and I was using the agreement as an excuse to keep me from thinking about what I want right now. I felt pressure from Jen because she really wants to get married, but I don't know yet. I love her, but I want to wait. You reminded me how beautiful marriage is and when and if I get married again, I want a true commitment and real marriage—no more divorce."

"Wow. That's courageous. I'm sure things are a bit tense right now. I hope she can understand."

"I was as honest as I could be with her. I think she saw the writing on the wall in your office. She's not happy, but she understands. I can't thank you enough for everything you said. If we do an agreement, you can bet it will be collaboratively. It's the only way that makes sense."

His final words were, "That consult meant more to us than we ever could have imagined. We had no idea lawyers like you existed or that a collaborative process was even available. Thank you for opening our eyes."

I did not get a client that day, but I established a meaningful relationship that I know will result in business because I connected with these people. Trust makes people remember you and call you.

I hold myself out as a collaborative professional because it connects with my authentic self. Raj and Jen met not just a family/divorce lawyer, but Brenda Baietto, a collaborative professional who values marriage, family, relationships, and quality representation.

Brenda A. Baietto established *Tampa Mediations*, a family law firm focusing on divorce and other types of family consults, mediation, and out-of-court legal representation, including collaborative law.

After years litigating marital dissolution cases and seeing the devastating effects of divorce litigation on families, she now uses her experience, skills, and resources to help clients more carefully engage on the issue of divorce, analyzing not only what it means to divorce but also how to move forward when divorce is inevitable and what process can best serve the family. Her clients know her as someone who is smart, creative, fair, and truly a counselor-at-law seeking the good for each spouse and the family.

Ms. Baietto has been a member of the Stann W. Givens Family Law American Inn of Court and is currently a member of the Family Law Section of The Florida Bar, Next Generation Divorce, and the International Academy of Collaborative Professionals.

Ms. Baietto frequently writes on the topic of catholic marriage, advocating to strengthen and value marriage between men and women in our society. She is also a faculty member for National Business Institute and Institute for Paralegal Education, speaking on the topic of divorce mediation.

She earned her B.A. degree with high honors from the University of South Florida and her J.D. degree from Marquette Law School, receiving the Jurisprudence Award and finishing as a Moot Court Semi-Finalist.

You may contact Ms. Baietto by e-mailing her at brenda@tampamediations.com.

Collaborative teams often consist of professionals other than just the attorneys, financial professional, and mental health professional. Accountants can offer insights that a financial professional in another specialty cannot. Realtors who specialize in buying and selling homes for divorcing couples understand the emotions and special issues that come with buying and selling major assets during a divorce. Real and personal property appraisers and business valuators can offer important information needed to settle a matter. Probate attorneys may be helpful for older or ill clients. Vocational experts may be necessary when issues arise regarding the amount and appropriateness of alimony. Child specialists are educated in the developmental stages of children and may be more skilled at crafting parenting plans than a mental health professional who concentrates in a different area. Mediators can assist when clients have reached a standstill on a tough issue.

If your team hits a roadblock in negotiations, consider whether an outside professional could help. – Ed. Note

EXPANDING THE PIE
BY ALLEN WEINZAPFEL

Frankie and Molly had been college sweethearts. When they married right after graduation, they were thrilled to start their life together. Molly taught school and Frankie began a fairly lucrative business selling used sports equipment. Both were successful, loved their jobs, and were ready to take the world by storm.

Eventually, they had two boys, two years apart. She kept working, but became the primary caregiver, while he remained the breadwinner.

Due to the stress of raising two young children, pursuing two full-time careers, and spending less quality time together, their relationship wore thin.

They began to argue daily over every little thing. Who changed the diapers and who forgot to pick up more of them from the grocery store. Who left the minivan a mess and whether they could afford a new car when the old one broke down once too often, stranding Molly on her way to school one morning. Who would get the kids ready for bed and when the dishwasher would get loaded.

Shortly after their tenth anniversary, Molly gave up. She borrowed money from her parents, got a lawyer, and petitioned for divorce. No one suggested a collaborative divorce to her, but her attorney seemed to be reasonable and cooperative. In fact, shortly after filing, he called Frankie's lawyer and told him what Molly's goals were. He asked the other lawyer to discuss Frankie's goals with him and to share them so that they might all "keep their eyes on the ball."

At first, Frankie felt blindsided and hurt. He had thought that they were happily married. Sure, they had their issues, but, until the day he was served with divorce papers (at work, in front of all his employees), he had no idea how miserable Molly was.

He hired the attorney his family recommended and trusted him to take care of it. Soon, he found himself in the middle of settlement negotiations with his soon-to-be-ex-wife, trying to sort out how to separate their intertwined lives. It made sense when his lawyer asked him to identify his goals and interests, so he worked hard to put aside his anger and to envision what his perfect life would look like in five years.

Nevertheless, when negotiating, he often grew indecisive about what he would compromise on. Sometimes he was generous, and other times, spiteful and unyielding. He disliked his negative emotions, but his anger made him lose sight of the fact that he was causing Molly's livid and sometimes spiteful reactions.

A friend of Molly's, who had suffered through a nasty divorce, advised her to make Frankie pay as much as possible. Luckily for Frankie and for their family, Molly didn't want to drag her kids or herself through such a messy ordeal. But his behavior was enough to make even the most even-tempered woman lose it.

When her lawyer heard about the friends' advice, he advised her to stop listening. "Your friend's divorce was *her* divorce, not yours. She was married to someone else, and you aren't the same person as she is. Anyway, if she's going to undermine my counsel, perhaps you don't need me. But I feel like all she's doing is living her anger at her ex through you, and that's not helpful."

Molly agreed and avoided sharing the details of her divorce with her friend until it was over.

Molly and Frankie's most contentious issue was the marital home, which had about $80,000 of equity in it. The question was who would get to stay and who would have to move out. Prior to learning of the divorce, Frankie had planned to remodel the kitchen and had signed a $20,000 contract for it. He used this as leverage to claim that he should stay. He took the position that Molly would have to pay half of the cost if she wanted to keep the house, knowing she didn't have the funds to do so.

As a schoolteacher, her income was less than a third of his. Because they had no other debt, she easily qualified for the refinance on the home. He had about $100,000 in assets in his retirement account, but she had no savings or retirement. Frankie was self-employed and they tended to owe money for taxes each year.

Because Molly had filed for divorce just after the first of the year, the income tax filing became part of their negotiations. Frankie had been about to file their tax return and had been complaining that they were going to owe Uncle Sam money. Because Molly was the one who wanted a divorce, he felt that she should have to pay half of the tax obligation. Therefore, her lawyer instructed Molly to contact her CPA to determine if she would have any tax liability if she were to file a tax return on her own.

Molly had just argued with Frank and was upset when she met with her accountant. "I've had it with him. I know you work for both of us, but we're getting divorced, and I need some financial advice."

Sonya was more surprised by Molly's blunt announcement than its content. She had been aware of the financial difficulties over the years and had seen plenty of divorces caused by debt.

She quickly offered some unexpected advice. "Are you already in court? If you are, get out; talk to Frankie about a litigation freeze and get yourselves a couple of collaborative attorneys who will agree not to go to court. You'll be far more likely to reach an agreement you guys can both live with."

Molly sat back a moment. "What's a collaborative attorney?" A small frown creased her forehead. "Are they more expensive?"

Sonya smiled. "They're *not* more expensive and the entire process is likely to cost far less than you'll spend in court." She pulled out her keyboard and started typing. "Do a little research online to find out all you want to know. Just Google "Collaborative Divorce Tampa Florida." You should find the statute and both practice groups of professionals, as well as the collaborative professionals who advertise it on their websites and write about it on their blogs.

"In the meantime, I'll give you both a list of attorneys I've worked with before, as well as the website address for my own practice group, in case you don't like any of these." Her printer started printing. "And I can act as your financial neutral if both you and Frankie agree." She handed Molly the paper.

"Okay. I'll look into it. In the meantime, can you answer a few questions for me?"

"Of course, I can, as long as you realize that I can't be your expert in any conflict you have with Frankie. But anything I can answer as a neutral, meaning I'm not aligned with either of you and I would tell Frankie the exact same thing, I will." Sonya beamed at Molly and got up to leave. "Let me get your file."

As she thumbed through her filing cabinet out in the hallway, Sonya hoped Molly would consider freezing the litigation. If they settled their divorce collaboratively, they were both far more likely to remain her clients, despite being divorced from each other. If they divorced in court, she would probably lose not just one but both, as she knew from years of experience dealing with divorce among her clientele. She'd even been called by a client more than once to testify against the other. That was *never* easy, treading the line between being respectful to the court but also being careful not to violate the accountant-client privilege between herself and that other spouse.

When Molly left Sonya's office, she called Frankie and asked him to agree to use Sonya as a neutral to help them problem solve their divorce. She hesitated about asking him to freeze the litigation, so she didn't. But he quickly agreed with a positive attitude and appeared to be open to working out a "win-win solution," as he put it.

Molly and Sonya then found that, if she filed her taxes by herself, even if she didn't claim either of their children or the mortgage interest credit, she would actually receive a tiny refund. Through the discussion with the CPA, she further determined that, if they filed together, Frankie would save about $10,000 in taxes that he would be required to pay if Molly were to file on her own.

Sonja explained it. "For years, taxpayers complained about the so-called marriage penalty when spouses earned similar salaries. When the two of them filed jointly, the combination income pushed them into a higher tax bracket than if they were single.

"Although Congress took steps to reduce that penalty, ensuring that the joint tax bill for married couples remains closer to the combined total they would have owed as single taxpayers, depending on their incomes, they can still be penalized for being married. But if they have substantially different salaries, the lower one can pull the higher one down into a lower bracket than his original tax bracket, reducing their overall taxes."

Sonya checked with Molly to be sure she was still following. She was. Sonya concluded, "So, in your case, your marriage reduced the tax burden for you both when you filed jointly. Getting divorced is going to drive Frankie's taxes back up again."

Sonya wondered if Molly would be vindictive. Too often, she had observed the spouse earning less react with glee that the higher-incomed spouse would be penalized. Molly's reaction was far from that, however.

She spoke of their goals in the divorce. "How can I maximize my goals while at the same time achieving Frankie's? If I make him an offer he can't refuse, all of us will be better off, right? Less time fighting, less angst, and less stress, right?"

Sonya loved this, an issue she could wrap her brain around for a positive result. She and Molly began to brainstorm.

While Molly was doing her own homework, Frankie was discussing the same issues with *his* attorney. Unhappily, he discovered that he would likely have to split his retirement fund with Molly, as it was a marital asset belonging to them both, pay her alimony and child support, *and* reimburse her for her half the equity in their home if he wanted to keep it.

He also discovered that he would owe about three times as much in taxes if she chose to file separately that year. "I guess I never really appreciated the value of the 'married, filing jointly' label."

So, when Frankie and Molly, their attorneys, and Sonya met to discuss these financial findings, Molly invited a mortgage professional to whom Sonya had introduced her. In discussing their options, Frankie was happy to learn that Molly had a creative solution that met each of their most important interests. She was willing to forgo alimony and to allow Frankie to keep all of his retirement—if she could have the home. Because she was asking for the home and all of the equity in it, she would do a cash-out-refinance on the home after the renovation to pay for the cost of the renovation, which Frankie had put on a credit card in just his name. She also agreed to file their tax return together to save him that $10,000.

At the final hearing, Frankie admitted to Molly that he never really wanted the marital home, he was just hurt. In fact, it was important to him that his boys stay there, and he was glad things had worked out the way they did.

Parties to a divorce often benefit from seeking guidance not only from their attorneys, but also from other professionals like accountants, financial planners, and mortgage specialists. Outside professionals can help them formulate creative settlements that most effectively satisfy their highest interests.

Allen Weinzapfel is a purchase lending manager who specializes in preparing home buyers with relationship-based mortgage counseling. He offers those who are purchasing or refinancing their real estate a personalized experience and a wealth of knowledge. He says "I especially focus on preparing my divorcing clients to make confident, informed decisions while, at the same time, alleviating the stress inevitably caused by the divorce process, coupled with the anxiety that results when they sell their most valuable assets and move from their homes."

Mr. Weinzapfel often consults with spouses after their divorces have been finalized. Because of this, he is all too well aware that a litigated divorce often results in the divorced persons being unable to purchase the homes that they would have liked, and that they could have purchased had they arranged their divorce more collaboratively. When he became aware that there was a collaborative alternative to a litigated divorce, and that he, too, could be an advisor to a collaborative divorce team, helping clients to achieve their housing dreams despite their divorces, he jumped on an airplane to Nashville, Tennessee to participate in the next available introductory collaborative training.

Contact Mr. Weinzapfel at allen.weinzapfel@loanflight.com.

Vocational consultants evaluate clients to determine: their employability; at what careers they might excel; whether they would benefit from additional training or education; and the reasonable income they can expect to earn. Vocational evaluation not only provides important information during a divorce but can also be an educational process for the client, who learns helpful information about himself and about the type of work that is appropriate for him based on his vocational skills, interests, and abilities. Clients with disabilities learn about the functional impact of their injuries or disabilities in relation to their career options. When support is at issue, a vocational evaluator can be a valuable resource to a collaborative team. – Ed. Note

THE VOCATIONAL CONSULTANT IN A COLLABORATIVE DIVORCE
BY CHRIS P. HALLISSEY, MA, CRC, IPEC AND
CINDY L. FISHER, MA, CRC, PVE, IPEC, ABVE

The central role of the vocational consultant is similar in litigated and non-litigated cases: to provide objective opinions about an individual's employability and earning capacity. These consultants contribute key knowledge about career development plans and the job market that can enhance a person's ability to establish a solid career. They, too, face unique challenges when helping divorcing couples because of the hostile nature of traditional divorce proceedings.

The need for collaboratively-informed vocational consultants has expanded with the growth of collaborative family law practice. The purpose of this chapter is twofold: first, to define the vocational consultant's role in the process; and, second, to discuss the value of these services in the collaborative approach in contrast to litigation. The following hypothetical case study shows how this works.

WHEN TO INVOLVE A VOCATIONAL CONSULTANT

Financial realities deepen the emotional impact of divorce. Many times, one spouse is the caregiver and the other is the breadwinner. Or one spouse puts aside a career to support the other's career goals. In the United States, about half of the married couples share the financial and domestic responsibilities.[4]

While the couple remains married, this works. Separation or divorce, however, changes both partners' needs and interests. Their former standard of living will differ. The primary financial provider will not have the same support at home, which may require a reduction in work hours. The caretaker may need to go to work to make ends meet. Restructuring family and social roles includes facing new financial burdens. The changes that follow a split are often the catalyst for alimony and spousal maintenance decisions.

In determining appropriate alimony or spousal maintenance awards, conflicting claims are often made about one or both spouses' ability and opportunity to work, earn, and contribute financially. At this point, a vocational consultant can step in to help. With specialized training in vocational assessment and rehabilitation counseling, the consultant is qualified to answer questions of employability and earning capacity, as well as to assist in return-to-work and work adjustment efforts.[5]

The following scenario shows the appropriate involvement of a vocational consultant. After 20 years of marriage, Mr. and Mrs. Jones separated and agreed to a collaborative divorce. By their second team meeting, they agreed to share equal custody of their two minor children. Mrs. Jones, a well-known business executive, had recently transitioned to a less-demanding position so she could spend more time with their children.

Mr. Jones, however, had not worked since before the birth of their first child thirteen years earlier and was by all definitions a stay-at-home father. Since the separation, Mr. Jones had moved into

---

[4] Employment Characteristics of Families Summary 2015. (2016, April 22). Retrieved from http://www.bls.gov/news.release/famee.nr0.htm.
[5] Kohlenberg, B. (2013). *Work and divorce: Vocational evaluation in family law*. Kohlenberg & Associates.

a two-bedroom apartment and obtained part-time employment as a substitute teacher.

During the third meeting, Mr. Jones claimed that his wife took a lower-paying job in an effort to reduce her potential alimony. She countered that he could easily return to work as a computer programmer. After further deliberation, the team suggested bringing in a vocational expert to clarify each one's earning power.

THE VOCATIONAL EVALUATION

In the constantly evolving world of work, job options are not always clear. For this reason, a vocational evaluation can help identify the individual's abilities and determine likely employment prospects.

The evaluation is an inherently collaborative process, involving the mutual participation of the evaluee and the vocational consultant. While intended to empower an individual to make informed decisions about career aspirations, the main goal in divorce proceedings is to determine an individual's employability and earning capacity.[6] In order to understand how a vocational evaluation helps, one must understand the following two concepts.

1. *Employability* is determined by developing a unique vocational profile for an individual based on skills, abilities, and interests. Other factors are the health, age, education, and employment history. The completed profile provides a clear picture of what jobs the evaluee is qualified for and best suited to perform. In economic terms, employability can be thought of as supply and is determined by identifying what the evaluee has to offer the labor market.

2. *Earning Capacity* matches the availability of local jobs and the salary the person can expect. Earning capacity does not always reflect an individual's past or current earnings, but reasonably estimates what she could make based on her employment potential. Earning capacity, a product of

---

[6] Robinson, R. H. (2013). *Foundations of forensic vocational rehabilitation.* New York, NY: Springer Publishing Company.

demand, is determined by identifying what the local market will pay for a particular position.

The evaluation typically involves an interview, a battery of tests, analysis of transferable work skills, and exploration of job opportunities. The consultant will usually request a resume, academic transcripts, earning records, and other documents.

In cases in which the evaluee has a disability, the consultant will review medical documentation to determine what work restrictions, if any, have been imposed. Vocational consultants have a comprehensive understanding of medical aspects of disability and are particularly competent in determining the employment potential of an individual with a disability.[7] This includes having extensive knowledge of assistive technologies, workplace accommodations, and legislative protections providing equal access to training and employment opportunities for individuals with disabilities.

The interview focuses on psychosocial factors that may affect employment. Specifically, the evaluee's physical and mental health, age, education, and employment history is discussed.[8] The interview also addresses avocational pursuits, such as hobbies, recreational involvement, and activities of daily living. A secondary goal of the interview is to establish rapport and address any concerns the evaluee may have about the evaluation process.

Vocational testing is used to assess the evaluee's current level of functioning and to identify how her vocational strengths can be applied in employment. Vocational testing can include the administration of any combination of interest, academic, intelligence, personality, and aptitude assessments. Prominent inferences about an evaluee's employment potential can be made based on testing results.[9]

---

[7] Rubin, S. E., & Roessler, R. T. (2008). *Foundations of the vocational rehabilitation process* (6th ed.). Austin, TX: Pro-Ed.

[8] Power, P. W. (2013). *A guide to vocational assessment* (5th ed.). Austin, TX: Pro-Ed.

[9] Drummond, R. J., & Jones, K. D. (2006). *Assessment procedures for counselors and helping professionals* (6th ed.). Upper Saddle River, NJ: Pearson/Merrill Prentice Hall.

Transferable skills analysis is another valuable tool. An individual's developed skills from past employment are analyzed to determine alternative jobs at which these skills can be used or to which they can be transferred.[10] This analysis gives the consultant valuable insight about the evaluee's physical, psychological, and intellectual tolerances. Transferable skills analysis is of particular importance when the evaluee has a disability precluding her from returning to her previous job.

Labor market data is used to determine the availability and projected employment trends of identified occupations of interest. Job listings, direct employer contact, and other collateral resources provide substantial evidence about available jobs and respective salaries in the relevant labor market.

Below is a summary of Mr. and Mrs. Jones' evaluations:

> Mr. Jones arrived for his appointment with an old resume. During the interview, he made it clear that he was uncomfortable with the idea of returning to work. When questioned, he said he dreaded the thought of working as a computer programmer because he was "too social to work behind a screen all day" and his testing confirmed this. After completing other tests and exploring numerous careers for which he qualified, he identified teaching as his top choice.

> He scored well academically and intellectually, providing further support for this goal. With the consultant's guidance, he excitedly explored the steps required to transition into a full-time position. Mr. Jones also compiled a list of other parents, teachers, and friends who would be able to help him.

> Mrs. Jones arrived with her 16-page *curriculum*

---

[10] Szymanski, E. M., & Parker, R. M. (2010). *Work and disability: Contexts, issues, and strategies for enhancing employment outcomes for people with disabilities.* Austin, TX: Pro-Ed.

vitae in hand. During the interview, she proudly listed her professional accomplishments, which included serving as the CEO of a large consulting firm and hosting annual leadership seminars for aspiring business professionals.

She talked about her decision to step down from her previous position and acknowledged the decrease in pay. While she was proud of her achievements, she regretted her lack of involvement with her children and feared losing custody completely. She detested the thought of returning to her former position, despite her capability in that field. At this point, it was evident that she was voluntarily underemployed and unlikely to return to a similar well-paying position.

ELEMENTS OF EMPLOYMENT PLANNING

Transitioning to a new job is stressful in and of itself, especially for someone who has been out of the workforce for a long time. A vocational consultant's guidance can help reduce this stress. In addition to the comprehensive evaluation report, consultants can develop an individualized plan for employment, enabling the individual to compete for better jobs.

While each person's needs are unique, effective job search efforts share common traits. They should be structured, persistent, and include multiple methods of outreach to potential employers.[11] An individual should spend at least 20 hours a week searching and should maintain a log tracking her efforts. Experts clarify the difference between passive and active job search methods.[12] Passive methods, such as forwarding the same email response to every job listing posted on Craigslist, are haphazard and without

---

[11] De Back, A. (2010). *Get Hired in a Tough Market: Insider Secrets to Find and Land the Job You Need Now.* New York: McGraw-Hill Professional.

[12] Labor force statistics from the current population survey (2015, October 8). Retrieved from http://www.bls.gov/cps/faq.htm.

specific intention. Active efforts are intentional, such as sending tailored resumes and cover letters to specific employers with appropriate openings.

A thorough plan includes the job seeker's networking resources and personal contacts, best defined by the age-old saying, "It's not what you know; it's who you know." While not detracting from an individual's skills and abilities, having an "in" with a potential employer is often more important than meeting every listed qualification.

A 2014 employment survey showed that 40% of job seekers landed their "favorite or best job" through personal connections.[13] The succeeding resources resulting in satisfactory employment were online social networking (21%) and online job boards (20%). With help from a vocational consultant, a person can utilize her existing network of contacts to jumpstart her job search.

Many state statutes require a specific plan for employment when rehabilitative alimony is awarded. The plan details the steps for an individual to acquire the education, training, or work experience necessary to establish self-support. It also lists the cost and length of time to complete the training, as well as potential employment afterward. Vocational consultants usually know about local programs and can provide further insight about post-completion employment prospects.

This additional preparation is most beneficial when an individual does not have the skills to seek a position paying more than minimum wage. Retraining also helps people whose job skills are obsolete or outdated because of technological advances.[14]

The vocational consultant shared his findings at the third team meeting. While Mr. Jones' bachelor's degree in information technology augmented his overall employability, he would need at least two years to update his skills as a computer programmer. The consultant produced various local job listings, all of which required candidates to have specific certifications and knowledge of recent technological advances.

[13] 2014 Jobvite Job Seeker Nation Study. (2014, June 19). Retrieved from http://web.jobvite.com/rs/jobvite/images/2014 Job Seeker Survey.pdf.
[14] Zunker, V. G. (2012). *Career counseling: A holistic approach* (8th ed.). Belmont, CA: Brooks/Cole.

Alternatively, the consultant recommended he seek full-time employment as a teacher. This choice aligned closely with Mr. Jones's tested and self-reported interests. Teaching would allow him to earn more money compared to other positions for which he currently qualified. Additionally, by the time he could pursue an entry-level job as a computer programmer, he could be earning a comparable salary as a third-year teacher.

The consultant emphasized that he had recently worked as a substitute teacher and had a network of contacts to help him transition to a full-time position. Furthermore, the results of intellectual and achievement testing supported the recommendation that he get a Temporary Educator Certificate. The consultant concluded by explaining that, with this certification, he would qualify for various full-time positions listed by the local school district and could begin working while he pursued the Professional Educator Certificate.

Then he explained why Mrs. Jones accepted the lesser-paying job. He also shared his impression that she was unlikely to return to a higher paying position. Despite this, the consultant confirmed she was, in fact, voluntarily underemployed and could reasonably increase her earnings by returning to her previous position, or one of similar prestige. The consultant produced various local job listings for which Mrs. Jones easily exceeded the hiring requirements. Considering her qualifications, professional accomplishments and business connections, the consultant concluded that Mrs. Jones could readily return to her previous level of earning with minimal difficulty.

VOCATIONAL CONSIDERATIONS IN INTEREST-BASED NEGOTIATION

The vocational evaluation process should help the evaluee gain a better understanding of her vocational strengths and how they fit into establishing a meaningful and rewarding career. Completing the evaluation should give the evaluee a deeper sense of self-awareness and more confidence in her abilities.

The caretaker who has been out of the workforce for many years may have been unaware of certain job options when he first requested alimony. The financial provider may not have fully considered how her earnings affect the family as a whole. These new insights can enhance the interest-based negotiations.

Following the third team meeting, Mr. Jones applied for the Temporary Educator Certificate. He also got an interview for a full-time position as a teacher's assistant at a local school where he substituted. The principal, who had arranged the interview, was familiar with Mr. Jones' work ethic and caring temperament. Mrs. Jones remained unwilling to consider returning to her previous position. She was, however, more understanding of her husband's financial needs and his frustration with her decision to step down from her job.

During the fourth team meeting, Mr. and Mrs. Jones explored various support options incorporating both of their interests. Mrs. Jones agreed to pay for his certification and provide additional support while he established himself as a teacher. In return, Mr. Jones, who had already taken significant steps towards this goal, agreed to seek a teaching position as soon as he was qualified. With his newfound passion for pursuing full-time teaching, and her understanding of how her decreased earnings affected the whole family, Mr. and Mrs. Jones finalized their divorce by the fifth collaborative team meeting.

COLLABORATION VS. LITIGATION
FROM THE PERSPECTIVE OF THE VOCATIONAL CONSULTANT

Neutrality is not a foreign concept to vocational consultants.[15] In lawyer language, consultants owe a duty of zealous advocacy on behalf of the truth, not the retaining client. As previously stated, this is true for the vocational consultant in litigated and non-litigated matters. As such, the retaining client may not receive favorable opinions from his or her consultant, depending on the facts of the divorce.

In a perfect world, a consultant would draw the same conclusions in a collaborative matter as in a litigated one. Moreover, if two consultants evaluated the same person, they, too, would come to similar conclusions about the evaluee's ability to work and earn.

---

[15] Commission on Rehabilitation Counselor Certification (2010). Code of professional ethics for rehabilitation counselors. Schaumburg, IL: Author.

But this doesn't always happen, largely due to various barriers inherent to the litigation process.

Valid information is critical. To form justifiable opinions about an individual's employability and earning capacity, a consultant must have facts that accurately reflect the evaluee's true level of functioning.

By nature of litigation, when one party requests a vocational evaluation, the other party may view the consultant as part of the "opposition." Consequently, and sometimes even under the instruction of counsel, an evaluee may maintain a defensive attitude, limit disclosures, and give less than a full effort. Skilled vocational consultants can identify inconsistencies and attitudinal manifestations that may affect the profile. However, even with these taken into consideration, the information used to formulate opinions and recommendations is still somewhat sullied.

Discrepancies may occur when each party retains a vocational expert, as often happens in litigation. The consultant who is viewed as an adversary is less likely to elicit the same level of evaluee participation afforded to the other consultant, resulting in different opinions. Not only is this practice futile in the majority of litigated cases, it also at least doubles the cost for vocational services. Moreover, while the additional and extended discovery is lucrative for attorneys and vocational consultants, it only hurts the parties financially.

CONCLUSION

Vocational consultants do not weigh in on who should get what or suggest what an evaluee should do with her life. Rather, the consultant is strictly limited to presenting unbiased and objective information about an individual's employability and earning potential. However, valuable insights often arise during the evaluation process that may help in the ensuing negotiations, if such negotiations are afforded. After all, the vocational evaluation is intended to be an opportunity for an evaluee to grow and develop a deeper sense of self-awareness.

These simplified representations point to the alternatives in litigated cases. If Mr. Jones had not confided in the vocational consultant, would he have ever considered teaching as a full-time career? Would Mrs. Jones' alimony have been determined based on her imputed earning potential without taking into consideration her rationale for accepting a decrease in pay? Would Mr. and Mrs. Jones have had the opportunity to consider each other's perspectives before final judgment? And how would their children have been affected if these decisions had been settled in court?

Christopher Hallissey holds a master's degree in rehabilitation and mental health counseling from USF. He is a nationally certified rehabilitation counselor and a Florida registered mental health counselor intern. He anticipates being granted full licensure in mental health counseling in 2017.

Mr. Hallissey is passionate about guiding individuals in accessing their potential to develop meaningful and rewarding careers. For the past three years, he has provided vocational counseling and evaluation services to individuals with disabilities attempting to return to the workforce.

Mr. Hallissey was recently appointed to the board of the Florida Rehabilitation Association and is active in numerous additional professional associations, including the National Rehabilitation Association, the International Association of Rehabilitation Professionals, and the American Mental Health Counselor's Association. He has received extensive training in employability and earning capacity assessment and is an aspiring vocational expert.

Mr. Hallissey worked in the foster care system and has seen firsthand the devastating effects divorce can have on children and their families. He also served as an emergency foster parent for an elementary student during the summer of 2015 and is a determined advocate for disenfranchised families.

Mr. Hallissey views collaborative divorce as the best alternative to traditional divorce proceedings. As a counselor, he feels strongly that collaborative divorce offers a way for families to preserve their integrity while working through a divorce.

Chris may be reached at ChrisVocationalConcepts@gmail.com.

Cindy L. Fisher has passionately provided vocational rehabilitation services for over two decades, helping countless individuals develop rewarding careers. She is the owner and director of vocational services at Vocational Concepts, which serves six counties in Florida.

Ms. Fisher is a graduate of the University of South Florida's Master of Arts program in rehabilitation and mental health counseling and currently maintains designations as a certified rehabilitation counselor and professional vocational evaluator.

Ms. Fisher is an active member of the International Association of Rehabilitation Professionals and the American Board of Vocational Experts. Ms. Fisher is recognized as a vocational expert by the Social Security Administration and regularly provides testimony in disability hearings. Additionally, Ms. Fisher provides vocational expert services in cases of marital dissolution and personal injury. Most recently, Ms. Fisher received training to provide vocational consultation services as an ancillary professional in collaborative divorce proceedings.

Ms. Fisher believes collaborative divorce is a smart alternative to litigation, and, most importantly, a necessary part of divorce healing. From her own personal experience with divorce, she knows that, if the collaborative process had been available years ago, her life might be different today, as children often feel the parental tensions which are never resolved after marital dissolution. A transition in which parents work together to communicate with reduced future tension is highly beneficial for the children. The collaborative process can provide a start to better communication and a civil ending to this most life-changing event.

Ms. Fisher's *curriculum vitae* can be viewed by visiting www.VocationalConcepts.com, and she can be reached at VocationalConcepts@gmail.com.

In many jurisdictions, divorcing spouses are required to take a parenting education course to learn how to better co-parent after a split. The course also teaches parents about the impact that divorce and parental conflict can have on children, as well as how to minimize the trauma. Parents learn how to talk about divorce in a healthy way with their children, as well as the emotional concerns and needs of children when their parents are divorcing. Parents gain insight into the legal procedure for resolving timesharing disputes and the availability of community services and resources to help divorcing parents. They learn about their financial responsibilities for their children and about the emotional experience of divorce, the stages of divorce, and the challenges facing a divorcing parent, including changing family relationships and dynamics.

While some clients are offended that they are required to attend such a course, if they learn even just one lesson that makes them a better parent, it's worth it. – Ed. Note

KNOW YOUR OPTIONS
BY SHAUN P. HOYLE, B.S.

As a parent educator for 14 years, I have worked with thousands of parents and families. For the past seven years, I have focused on divorcing families, teaching the Florida state-mandated class, "Parent Education and Family Stabilization." Additionally, for the last five and a half years, I have taught the High Conflict Diversion Program at least three times a week. This work, as well as experiencing the end of my own 20-year marriage, has sensitized me to the legal, financial, and emotional issues implicated for families undergoing the divorce process.

I have never met a parent who intentionally wished to hurt his or her children. Parents do the best they can with the tools they have in their parenting toolboxes. Conflict in families, however, is detrimental to the mental, emotional, academic, and social development in children. As an educator, I provide information and perspective, allowing parents to see that their actions may not generate the results that they want.

I have been a member, a board member, and an officer of the Twelfth Judicial Circuit Family Court Professional Collaborative, Inc. (FCPC) since 2009. The purpose of FCPC is to improve processes for resolving family disputes through development and utilization of a wide variety of dispute resolution methods, educational resources, and appropriate affordable services in the Twelfth Judicial Circuit of Florida.

FCPC provides leadership and an interdisciplinary forum for communication, collaboration, education, and innovation among professionals and other interested persons who are concerned with the legal process, the unique interest of children, family dynamics, and the safety of adults and children. Participation in FCPC has allowed me to understand firsthand the dilemmas presented to the legal, financial, and mental health professionals concerning separating and divorcing couples. Upon hearing parents recount their perceptions of their own situations, my heart aches for them— and for their innocent children. I understand how and what they are experiencing. This perspective is invaluable.

While teaching the Parent Education and Family Stabilization class, I have worked with many parents with vastly different viewpoints. Since becoming collaboratively trained in May 2013, I have added collaborative process education to my classes. Until that time, the proudest and most content parents were those who worked out their paperwork with the assistance of one attorney or a mediator.

The parents I meet who use the collaborative process appear many times happier than those settling with a mediator or utilizing one attorney. Prior to the collaborative process gaining traction in Florida, these parents would have likely hired litigating attorneys. However, parents who choose the collaborative way hope to resolve their issues outside of the courtroom. They see that the process will provide an end result that will bolster, not damage, their self-esteem. Rather than experiencing a hostile divorce process that drains energy and damages self-worth, the collaborative process helps empower and raise children who learn how to handle adversity, an important life skill obtained through a difficult life lesson.

I typically have at least one collaborative couple attend each class, and the number is increasing. That warms my heart.

After one recent class, I overheard a conversation between an apprehensive mother involved in a litigated divorce, Sue, and a light-hearted collaborative mother, Pam.

Sue commented, "Pam, you seem so relaxed. Aren't you upset and stressed about your divorce?"

Pam responded, "Well, I'm not happy about it, and it's not what I want. We're using the collaborative process that our instructor just taught. We weren't on the same parenting page or in agreement with many other issues. But I've learned so much from my collaborative team about coping with divorce, communication skills, and co-parenting after divorce. So even though I'd prefer that things had turned out a different way, I'm content about my future as a co-parent with my children's father."

Sue seemed in awe. "Wow. I'm definitely not having that experience. All we do is fight while the attorneys just rack up fees. But isn't collaborative divorce even more expensive? What's the process like?"

Pam replied, "My children's father, Scott, and I each met twice with our attorneys and a facilitator, and once with a financial professional. After the third meeting, I felt frustrated because it seemed like everyone was just having these casual conversations and nothing was being done.

Sue interrupted, "Nothing? No written agreements?"

She replied, "No, and so I voiced my concern to my attorney. My attorney shared that during the collaborative process, the team works to gather the information from the divorcing couple regarding our goals for our emotional, financial, parental, and physical needs. It takes some time for everyone to understand and get comfortable with one another. The process is transparent, and people can be vulnerable. It's very different when compared to litigation."

"So how much longer did it take?"

"Not long after that. During the next meeting, we began putting everything together, and we were done shortly afterward."

"How long were the meetings?"

"We never went over three hours. Most of them were only two hours."

"So how long did it take you to reach an agreement?"

"Six months, give or take."

"Wow, my attorney has said that's how long I may wait for our next court date." Sue seemed to mull over Pam's comments. "That sounds so much better than what my children's father and I are going through. I need to talk with him about changing to the collaborative process." Sue looked as though a weight had been lifted from her shoulders as she walked out of class with a smile on her face.

What a gift Pam gave Sue—the hope that the legal process can be much easier for a family's financial, relationship, and emotional wellbeing!

Often, parents believe that they have to "get along" to utilize the collaborative process. In fact, many adversarial issues are resolved in the collaborative process instead of being aired out in public and in the courtroom.

It is vitally important to create a loving and emotionally safe environment for your children, which includes laughing and enjoying life. The period of divorce is a "chapter" in both the parents' and children's lives. How parents handle it impacts their children for the rest of their lives.

My passion about our future generations leads me to repeat a couple of topics. I encourage you to stop using "ex" to describe anyone. The word's negative connotation conveys disrespect about someone's mother or father. Instead, please use "child," "daughter," "son," a child's name, "Mom," "Dad," "Mother," or "Father." If not in the children's presence, the term "parenting partner" is acceptable. I also recommend using "child-sharing time" or "Mom/Dad time" instead of "time-sharing." They are children, not condos. Avoid the terms "babysitting," "visiting," and "spending time." Finally, equalize the children's homes by no longer saying "Mom's house" or "Dad's house." Either refer to homes with a positive physical description, like the "yellow house," the address, or the area; or refer to them as "your house with Mom/Dad."

Furthermore, children read parents' body language and tone of voice. Never have a conversation about the other parent or the children when they can hear you. They imagine the other half of the conversation when you're on the phone, and they are rarely accurate. Keep your differences between the adults.

I encourage *all* parents to investigate and explore their resources for court-less processes, especially the collaborative process. Working outside of legal limitations, those that best serve your family will always be most beneficial.

Shaun Hoyle is a certified parenting educator, coach, and founder of Life Lessons of Manasota, LLC. As a director of the International Network for Children & Families, Ms. Hoyle trained instructors to teach the Redirecting Children's Behavior (RCB) course with author Kathryn Kvols, from whom she received her certification in April 2002.

Ms. Hoyle is the proud mother of two sons and has lovingly and successfully implemented RCB in her own home since 1997. Now that they are both off to college, she spends her time enlightening other families about how to find peace and harmony.

Since April 2002, Ms. Hoyle has helped hundreds of parents and professionals learn and refine the tools for parenting. In a safe, relaxed environment, she helps to bring growth and understanding through her command of the RCB theories, personal experience, and anecdotes.

Ms. Hoyle began teaching the four-hour "Parent Education & Family Stabilization" course for the 12th Judicial Circuit in January 2009. Recognizing the need in her judicial circuit for a program for those parents stuck in high-conflict relationships, in March 2009, Ms. Hoyle received her certification to teach the "High Conflict Diversion Program."

Ms. Hoyle has been an active member of the Family Court Professional Collaborative (FCPC) since 2009 and presently serves as secretary on the board of directors. She presented at the FCPC conferences in October of 2011, 2012, and 2015.

In August 2009, Ms. Hoyle received her instructor certification to teach the "Redirecting for a Cooperative Classroom" course so that she can train professionals working with children in classroom settings.

Ms. Hoyle received her certification as a collaborative facilitator in May 2013. She has attended additional advanced collaborative trainings with Ron Ousky, Forrest "Woody" Mosten, and Joryn

Jenkins.

Ms. Hoyle is a member of the IACP, FACP, AFCC, and Next Generation Divorce. She is the proud recipient of the 2015 "NGD Member of the Year" award.

Ms. Hoyle received her Bachelors of Science degree in Marketing from Florida Southern College in Lakeland, FL. She has resided in the Sarasota/Bradenton area since 1978. Feel free to sign up for her FREE parenting newsletter on the front page of her website. If you would like to reach Ms. Hoyle, contact her at Shaun@LifeLessonsOfManasota.com.

People undergoing divorce are typically grieving and need special attention, especially during stressful, life-changing occasions. Selling the family home, one filled with so many memories, both good and bad, can be especially upsetting and emotional. It may be the place where the couple fell in love, their first home as a married couple, or the place where their babies took their first steps. It is also the place of many heated arguments, perhaps where an affair took place, or where physical violence occurred.

The family home holds so many memories, so when it must be sold in a divorce, having a Realtor® who specializes in helping people buy and sell their homes pursuant to divorce can make the process a bit easier on the couple. – Ed. Note

DIVORCING YOUR HOME
BY RANDE FRIEDMAN

"Where am I going to live?" is one of the most common questions for divorcing individuals. Real estate transactions are filled with anxiety, even for a unified couple; stress escalates when couples separate. While litigation over who should get the home can increase tension, collaborative professionals work to reduce that anxiety. A financial neutral and facilitator work with the couple to create a transparent setting, to alleviate these issues, rather than to intensify them. Having a collaboratively-trained Realtor® involved keeps the spirit and goals of the collaborative divorce process on track.

TOM AND AMY'S STORY

A collaborative attorney recently contacted me to assist in her client's divorce. The couple, Tom and Amy, owned a home, and after the financial neutral provided the values for their assets and the amounts of their liabilities, they decided to sell it. Doing this before the divorce is finalized provides the best way to determine the home's value for equitable distribution purposes.

My first meeting with them took place at their house. After our introductions, they gave me a tour and walked with me around the property. I tried to alleviate their insecurities by taking a slow pace. Walking briskly would not give them time to process emotionally that they would be leaving this home they bought together.

I scheduled the first meeting when their two young sons were at a scouting meeting. I know from experience that parents view their children's rooms with pain when they discuss the sale of their home. By not having children present, the parents avoid adding more confusion and feelings of insecurity to the process. Amy became a little teary-eyed when she saw the pencil markings of the boys' growth on the doorframe; Tom tried, unsuccessfully, to hide his emotions.

After the tour, I asked them to sit on the same side of the kitchen table opposite me to discuss the sale. It is especially important to counter a divorcing couple's natural tendency to sit opposite each other. Sitting them together subconsciously emphasizes that they must work together in their common goal to sell their house in a reasonable amount of time for the highest price possible.

I explained, "I will be neutral as I represent you as equals during the sale process. While I will not divulge any confidential information to buyers and their agents, I will be transparent to your collaborative team."

They nodded in understanding and agreement. I asked them to sign a one-page, one-paragraph Florida broker form stating my duties and obligations. Amy smiled at the obligation, which declared my obedience.

We watched my marketing plan presentation and discussed the needed repairs to make the property more desirable to buyers. Even though it would benefit Tom and Amy to complete the improvements, as it would increase the net proceeds they would realize from the sale, there is always a tendency for divorcing couples to avoid spending energy and money when they are leaving a home. A specialized divorce Realtor® should monitor the list on a consistent basis.

We then reviewed my initial market analysis. Because it was only based on my examination of the home's exterior, it needed honing. In addition to the revised comparative market analysis, I ordered (at my expense) a broker's price opinion (BPO). A BPO, done by a third party independent licensed real estate professional, is a more thorough analysis of the current market conditions. While less in-depth than a full appraisal, banks and other institutions use these reports to determine what price a property may sell for in the next 30 days. This extra report is important for several reasons: it helps to generate a sound listing price, it gives another analysis to the sellers, and most importantly, it provides supporting evidence in case another attorney wants to know how the listing/selling price was derived.

The next step was to discuss the logistics of showing the house and the children's involvement. I asked Tom and Amy to fill in the times on a paper calendar when they were able to have the house shown. Having them physically write down the times commits them on a deeper level than a verbal agreement. At times during the divorce process, a spouse may hesitate to continue. Some passive-aggressive spouses will refuse to let the property be shown to delay the sale or to get revenge against the other spouse. Being able to show the spouse that he agreed to a schedule in his own handwriting helps to resolve the issue.

They were becoming a bit anxious, so I wrapped up our first meeting. I reviewed what they needed to accomplish with the house preparation and gave them a tentative scheduling for the BPO agent and the professional photographer. I clarified their contact information and told them I would communicate with both of them.

"I'll send all correspondence to both of you. Even if it concerns showing the house and Amy is the only one who needs to approve the time, I'll email or text both of you. When phone conversations must take place, it should be conference calls between the three of us. And, if your collaborative team requests information or updates from me, I'll provide it. Transparency is key to achieving a successful outcome."

Two weeks later, Amy emailed me. The house repairs were nearly complete so I could schedule the BPO agent and the photographer. I had the BPO completed first so that I could review the results with Tom and Amy while I was at the home with the photographer. I accompany the photographers to all the photo shoots because, even though they are seasoned residential professionals, we stage the house, and I ensure that the special property features are shot.

Later, at the kitchen table, I gave each spouse copies of the BPO and my revised comparative market analysis. Because the house was located in a large and desirable subdivision, there were plenty of similar properties to contrast and compare to their home. The BPO was exactly the price for which the house should sell. We discussed what a smart listing price would be, with my explanation on timing. Because it is always best to have the transaction closed before the divorce is finalized, both for ease of moving and to be able to have a clear understanding of the proceeds, I suggested that Tom and Amy agree to a listing price very close to the BPO price. This strategy has been proven to bring multiple offers from better-qualified buyers. Tom and Amy agreed, and I told them I would place the house on the market as soon as I received the photos from the photographer.

As I expected, when I placed the house on the market a few days later, Tom called me, panicked. "I'm not sure if I'm ready."

I reminded him, "I know how difficult it is to sell your home during a divorce, but remember our agreement that you, Amy, and I all communicate together. I'll stop by the house tonight with the completed listing campaign for your review. We can discuss your concerns then."

Because this isn't unusual, I was well prepared when I met with them that night. When they saw the beautiful multimedia presentation that I would promote online and in print, they both got excited again. As they reminisced over the photos, I steered the comments towards the future.

Along with photos and articles about the house that I was going to post online, I brought my guidelines and questionnaire for finding new places for them each to live. Because they had both reported the expected net proceeds from the house sale to the collaborative team, we knew the amounts of each of their housing budgets.

I then segued into the smaller homes and townhouses within the boys' current school district. I limited the selections to the same quality level as the home they were leaving, just smaller. This made it easier for them to understand that moving wasn't going to change their lifestyles dramatically.

I arranged to meet each spouse separately to look at properties. When looking for new places to live, communications are kept one-on-one and restricted to matters about the new houses.

Amy wanted a maintenance-free townhouse with the best layout located closest to the school. Fortunately, there was a wonderful townhouse community within the subdivision, and there were several homes on the market. She submitted an offer with an addendum stating that the purchase would only occur when the sale of the marital home closed and that we would close at the same title company office where the marital home sale closed.

The first townhouse owners couldn't meet those conditions, but happily, the second and equally nice townhouse's seller accepted. When I took Amy and her sons for a second look, the boys gleefully explored the house and the backyard, with only a minor squabble over who got which bedroom.

When Tom and I looked at houses a few days later, he clarified that he'd rather rent initially. We stopped at a Starbucks, logged onto MLS, and researched townhouse and condominium rentals. A new apartment complex seemed to be a good fit, so we drove over to check it out. After the leasing agent showed us around and explained the very advantageous opening specials, Tom chose a unit with a waterfront view. Because the complex offered the first month's rent free, Tom decided that it would be easier for everyone if he moved out before the house sold. There was a one-car garage included with the apartment, which would relieve the house of some clutter.

We received showing requests the first day the house was listed on MLS, Zillow, Realtor, and numerous other websites. With the boys at school, Amy allowed me to line up multiple buyers and agents. Due to the attractive photos and descriptions, along with the realistic listing price, three offers came in that same day. The first offer was from a buyer who contacted me directly through my website marketing, the second was brought to us from a reputable agent in the community, and the third was from an online broker.

Tom, Amy, and I met at the house the following evening to review the offers. Before the meeting, I had called the mortgage lenders that each buyer was using. I confirmed that all the necessary due diligence had been performed by the lenders to ensure that the buyers would be approved for the mortgage loan. I had done this previously with the buyer with whom I was working. During our meeting, I carefully explained all of the terms and conditions of each offer and the strength of the buyer's capability to obtain financing.

The first buyer, the offer I had submitted, was for the full price, with a credit from the seller paying some of the buyer's closing costs. This purchase had to be made with an FHA loan, requiring only 3.5% down payment from the buyer. This was a typical offer, and the buyer was well qualified for a pre-approval.

The second buyer from the agent who I personally knew came in slightly lower, not asking for any closing costs and with conventional financing at 25% down. They were also well qualified, as was the bank from which they were obtaining the loan.

The third offer was considerably lower, with an FHA loan pre-approval from an online lender that had no office in town, so we focused on the two stronger offers.

A major advantage of the first offer was that, because the buyer was my customer, I would know exactly how the loan process was proceeding. Disadvantages were the weaker low down payment and more regulated FHA loan requirements. The second offer was stronger in the financing criteria, but weaker in the actual price the sellers would receive. I suggested that they counter the second offer with an amount closer to full price, as they had genuinely received that from another buyer. They agreed, and I sent the adjusted and initialed contract back to the agent, Gwen.

The next morning, Gwen called and gave me a verbal acceptance and sent the buyer's initialed documents back the same day. Even though I was losing out on the buyer's side of the commission, it certainly was better for Tom and Amy, and that is what matters most. I also told Gwen, the buyer's agent, that the agent from Amy's townhouse would contact her to ensure that a contract was in place and that the outcome should be successful. It is important in situations when there is a contingency on a buyer selling a house in order to purchase a new one that everyone communicates openly and regularly.

The inspections and appraisals on both Amy's townhouse purchase and the sale of the marital home went well, with only a few minor repairs needed.

As a specialist in selling divorcing couples' properties, I can honestly say that the difference between the collaborative process and litigation is simply amazing. While litigating brings out the worst in people and results in an undercurrent of animosity between the adversarial parties, collaborative clients are far calmer and more respectful to each other and to the professionals who are assisting them. Tom and Amy genuinely wanted this phase of their divorce to have the least negative effect on their boys, and they were successful in that goal.

It was a pleasure working with a couple of experienced Realtors®, as well as a title company that is knowledgeable in divorce matters. Closing went smoothly, and when I handed Amy the keys to her new home, she was happy. What was even nicer, and rarely seen in a litigated divorce, was that Tom was there to lend support and to help her move.

Rande Friedman, a White Glove House® Realtor, is an accomplished real estate agent in the Tampa Bay area. He has over a decade of experience in the industry with an expertise in helping divorcing people with their real estate needs. As an affiliated member of the

Hillsborough County Bar Association, Mr. Friedman is able to attend classes, workshops, and training seminars that are not available to general realtors.

Mr. Friedman is also a member of the International Academy of Collaborative Professionals and the local practice group Next Generation Divorce. The IACP and the local practice group provide ongoing training in the collaborative divorce process, which is essential when dealing with couples going through a sensitive and challenging real estate transaction.

Contact Mr. Friedman at whiteglovehouse@gmail.com.

www.ingramcontent.com/pod-product-compliance
Lightning Source LLC
Chambersburg PA
CBHW052130270326
41930CB00012B/2826